#2020
VISION

#2020 VISION

UNBOUND PERSPECTIVES FROM A YEAR LIKE NO OTHER

CURATED BY
THE UNBOUND PRESS

ISBN: Ebook 978-1-913590-20-8
ISBN: Paperback 978-1-913590-19-2

The Unbound Press
www.theunboundpress.com

Hey unbound one!

Welcome to this magical book brought to you by The Unbound Press.

At The Unbound Press we believe that when women write freely from the fullest expression of who they are, it can't help but activate a feeling of deep connection and transformation in others. When we come together, we become more and we're changing the world, one book at a time!

This book has been carefully crafted by both the contributors and publisher with the intention of inspiring you to move ever more deeply into who you truly are.

We hope that this book helps you to connect with your Unbound Self and that you feel called to pass it on to others who want to live a more fully expressed life.

With much love,
Nicola Humber

Founder of The Unbound Press
www.theunboundpress.com

CONTENTS

FOREWORD

....

As I sit down to write this, I'm staying in an Airbnb in Rochester, New York. In two days, I will leave this city that I have called home for the last 3+ years to return to the UK. And this seems to be one in a LONG line of plot twists that 2020 has presented each of us with, not just individually of course, but collectively.

'We're all in this together' – I know this is a phrase that attracted derision at times during 2020 and certainly many people have been impacted much more adversely than others during this most shocking of years. The patriarchal and white supremacist structures that we live within have been more apparent than ever. But one thing is for sure, you'd be hard-pushed to find anyone who didn't experience some kind of deep transformation in 2020. So, in that sense, we have all been in 'it' together – trying to find our way through the uncertainty, the chaos and sometimes downright terror.

It's funny, because for the past few years, I'd been talking about how the 'old ways are crumbling to make way for the new.' I could feel that this was happening. I would tell my husband, Mr H, a super-logical engineer, that 'something big' was coming, something was going to happen that would change EVERYTHING.

'How do you know?' he would ask. 'What evidence do you have for that??' And all I had was my gut, a sense of knowing.

As we moved into 2020, it seemed that there was this pervasive feeling of optimism – it was going to be a breakthrough year. Maybe that's how we always feel about a new year, but this one felt different. And boy was it!

For me personally, 2020 was absolutely a breakthrough year in many different ways. I lost my dad at the beginning of the year just before the impact of COVID fully hit and I was grateful to be at his bedside in the UK for the last days before he journeyed on from this world.

My heart broke open. I felt love like never before. Preparing me for what was to come.

Because dad chose not to have a funeral and instead donated his body to medical science, I flew back to the US much sooner than I may otherwise have done after his death and arrived just a few days before lockdown hit.

Back in the arms of Mr H, my concept of living unbound broke open. Could I feel free and fully expressed when I was confined to the four walls of my house? The answer, I discovered, was more than ever.

As the world stopped and we all adjusted to a new way of being, more and more womxn started to connect with me, saying, 'This is the time to write my book!'

My business broke open. New authors streamed into the Unbound Writing Mastermind I host and signed with The Unbound Press. The sense of urgency and expansion was palpable.

George Floyd was murdered and more layers of these fucked-up structures I'd been living within, putting up with, upholding, became crystal clear.

My commitment to anti-oppression broke open. This murky soup that we've been swimming in for so long we can't even see it, like goldfish in a bowl. No more.

And as we moved towards the end of the year, what stood out for me were the themes of community, collaboration and co-creation.

My heart breaks open, over and over again, as I realise that we were never meant to do 'this' alone; this life, this journey, these books even. We are all in this together.

When we come together, we become more.

Each of us has a unique and vital part of this collective puzzle we're putting together right now.

That's why it felt important to bring this book together – *#2020VISION* serves as a kind of time capsule, a way we can look back and hear different perspectives of a year that really was like no other (although as I write this, of course, I have NO idea what 2021 and beyond will bring. How is it over there, dear reader?)

I'm fascinated by both the very personal stories and collective themes that are shared in this book. What a privilege it has been to be the first to read them. You are in for a treat!

So, as you dive into #2020VISION now, I invite you to imagine you're in circle with each of the writers here. One by one they step forward to share their stories, their learnings, their breakthroughs.

Clearing the way for what's next.

To be continued…

Always, unbinding
Nicola Humber

Founder of The Unbound Press

UNEARTHING THE TRUTH
by Natalie Farrell

....

Meet me at the gate Sister
Leave your shoes where they are
And feel your flesh smile

Tread lightly toward me Sister
Piercing gently through your shield
And surrender soft heartedly

Sit down with me Sister
Naked now with your truth
And passionately stir out that façade

Conjure with me Sister
Stoke your potent wildness
And forgive the flames of fear

Let go with me Sister
Tend to those tamed wounds
And revive them in all their glory

Float with me Sister
Into the delicious untamed edges

And let's play with magic

An ode to my unbound sisters
For believing in me, listening to me and
encouraging me to set
alight the flame of my soul's purpose

....

Look into my eyes. There you will see the reflection of 100 souls dancing and moving freely to the beat of their hearts. Pure unadulterated energy being released and witnessed for all to enjoy. Look closer my friend and you'll hear the warmth of raw flamenco tones wrapped in the rugged Andalusian hills.

Welcome to my memory of January 1st 2020. My husband, Freedy, and I had chosen to celebrate the new year at a festival held at Wakana Lakes, close to our home in Southern Spain. We wanted to enter into 2020, eating good food, enjoying new experiences and drinking in life under the stars rather than waking up into the new year with the inevitable hangover!

Wakana Rebirthing Festival allowed us space to reconnect and rejoice in the simplicity of nature. The weekend itinerary certainly pushed my spiritual boundaries – with ancient cacao ceremonies, ecstatic dancing, and sweat lodges up for the taking – I walked into the weekend with an open mind and body.

Seeing the new year in with 12 beats on a shamanic drum and eating the traditional 12 Uvas (grapes) surrounded by soulful people, felt right. YES! YES! YES! I could feel my body happy and grateful as I danced wildly in this celebration.

Embracing our inner tribal instinct

As I recall this memory, the pure essence of being high on life is bringing me to tears. Being human is incredible but we are flawed. We love to find the easy route – following like sheep, flocking to fun, rather than stepping up in the face of truth and embracing our inner tribal instinct.

So many experiences in this life are shadowed with a dampening of our natural spirit. Society has taught us that, to have a good time we need to enhance our mood with drink, drugs and sex. These enhancers can be OK when used in a loving way. Yet they can tarnish the glow of our inner yearnings, hiding our flaws and imperfections, rolling in the shame of us.

But what about if you allowed your natural hormones to do their thing?

What if you raised your vibrations through a clear vessel until you were naturally bouncing on top of life?

This is how I moved into 2020 – Free Flowing

I haven't always been in alignment with the free-spirited part of myself. In my early 20's I was laden down with bulimia and self-hatred. In my late 20's you would have found me time and time again in the wrong relationship, smiling through gritted teeth, happy to be there as it was better than being alone. And until the age of 33 I was in a job I liked yet didn't tingle my creative juices into fruition.

Cutting into untamed edges

On New Year's Day with my heart crushed against 100 others in the biggest group hug of my life I knew that the free spirit in me was ready to rise. A switch had been turned on. Reignited.

The delicious untamed edges of my light were back with me and ready to start making magic.

I felt untamed.

I felt abundant with joy.

I felt rebirthed.

A hostage in our own homes

My 2020 vision initially had been to apply for a Ted Talk with Charlotte my blood sister. However, 2020 had other visions for me! With my façade shield dissipated, I was opened to receive new ways of being. At long last I could thrive on my intuitive guidance.

Shedding and shifting is never easy for any of us. When we make a decision to change and be more at one with ourselves, we enter into unknown territory. In many decisions around self-change, we have a choice in the timing, but not this year.

As the world went on a break, the 2020 vision we had at the beginning of the year soon emancipated into a mirror of questioning. Our lives were being reflected back at us in the strongest way, like prana life force itself being injected back into our veins. We had a choice – to go with the flow or to go with the fear.

Moving deeper into the silence

At the heart of these challenges, the strength of human kindness and integrity began to rise. Communities began to support one another, families reinstating their time spent together, people's true voices awakening. I saw this as an invitation for humans to revolt. Mother Earth was showing up for us like never before, spewing up our inner demons, showing us, we were ready to own our truth and start standing in the shoes of who we were born to be.

Take the fear road or take the truth road.

Which one did you choose?

Whichever one you chose, there would be twists and turns, tears, sweat, riots, loneliness, laughter, for this time in our lifetime we were in a Global Pandemic. We were being shown the impact that our ignorant daily consumerism has on the planet too. As the stillness stayed, footage of wild animals moving closer to share our space was a beautiful reminder that we are cohabiters not proprietors.

Bird dances and song could be enjoyed as the skies remained free from human flight. Never before had we felt so close to our fellow human beings as all of us sat in our homes. Conforming to save lives and reduce risk of infection. As people scratched at the surface of their lives, love and connection began to resurface within their heart's desires.

A wake-up call. Waiting to be welcomed. A once in a lifetime chance for super growth. To unearth our soul's desires. Welcome in our soul tribe. Stop thinking and start our own soul revolution.

New ways of being

I remember the moment when we were told in March that we had to stay in our house for two weeks. I was walking along the beach with Freedy and our dog Rocket. It was a late Sunday afternoon, and the beach was bare of human life.

I recall saying out loud, "There is no way anyone is making me stay in my house for two weeks! How dare they!"

A week later having understood the severity of the objective of lockdown I was totally and utterly immersed in creating a new way of being. Two weeks later, I was loving my new routine. One month later, I was very happy only leaving my home once a day for a 30-minute dog walk.

Six weeks later, I had settled into a new work routine. Actioning to do lists which had sat untouched for months and as my routine began to flow so did the work opportunities.

I clearly remember feeling it was my time to serve. To be there for my community and to build a community so I could reassure and use my teachings to keep people calm. I had already made the decision in 2015 when returning from my yoga teacher training to run my business online. So online living was comfortable for me.

A dose of cosmic love:

When we make a decision to develop ourselves, we are taking a lifelong path towards change. When we then decide to be a teacher it is our job to share. When illuminated with the magic of our intuitive wisdom we begin to remember a deep knowing inside.

The information you are being delivered is not yours to keep.

I was being guided to share my teachings. If all the work and studying I had done prior to 2020 was my foundation, then 2020 was to become my platform. I had wriggled away many a time from talking openly about being an intuitive so when I received a phone call to be a radio presenter on Wellbeing Radio, I of course instantly said YES!

This opportunity appeared to open a portal for me. And I began to meet and connect with like-minded souls. I was finally part of a tribe who understood me. Who got me!

My Yoga practice taught me to embrace an integrated and holistic approach to life. I had learnt too that Yoga is not about competition and comparing ourselves to others but about welcoming each other's differences. So, I knew I was safe to be vulnerable as I began to speak my truth across the radio waves.

I found myself chatting with high priestesses, goddesses, creatrixes from across the globe, sharing the wisdom of their wise women and light. It was easy, and for the first time in my life, truly flowing. This opening was meant to be as thousands of people tuned in to my show waiting to hear how to create a life – fuelled by their soul.

Untying the knots

As I recorded my show each week, I began to believe in my powers. I also began to make decisions which I had been procrastinating over for months or years in some cases!

One morning on a dog walk these words came through so clearly to me;

I am ancient intelligence which has been upon this planet many times before and I am here now in this time of energetic evolution to guide the ones who want to rise away from suffering and wake up to a lighter way of living.

As well as these powerful words, a whoosh of energy ran through my veins. It was the second affirmation from my intuition. Showing me that this message was my truth.

Let's get naked

In order to evolve, we must care more for the ripple of change; rather than for the stone that created it.

Showing up in the world as who you were born to truly be is like showing up at a party, walking in with huge amounts of confidence and then realizing you have forgotten to put your clothes on!

Exposed

Vulnerable

Naked

As the day you were born. Kicking, screaming and crying your way into the world. To wake up in this way is a rebirthing.

The moment when you are truly ready to wake up to who you were born to be, the waves of uncertainty and doubt begin to part, the flickers of thoughts of being judged disperse and the river of truth runs wildly with abandonment.

If you keep hiding away in your little holes of self-doubt, self-criticism, self-loathing, you will only be annoyed at yourself. The new skin is forming. The wild woman within, unleashing.

Unearthing your truth

Showing up in 2020 began for me with weekly online yoga classes. Everyone switched to Zoom, but I wanted to create a non-exclusive community. Offering free resources to all.

In 5 days, my private yoga Facebook group grew from 60 people to 380 people. They were eager to sit with me and find some clarity and focus. In the first session, I remember how powerful and emotive it was.

Let me explain how my work comes to me;

I tune in to the energy of the class. I tune in to the energy of the day and I trust that I am creating a session which flows along with the needs of the participants.

In our first session, I felt the overwhelm of disconnection from the outside world. And guided the 15 people in the class to sit with me in a circle and to hold hands. As we held hands, I felt again that overpowering whoosh of energy.

With my intuition holding me, affirming again that I had led them in the correct way for that moment, shivers appeared all over my body. The shivers are a daily occurrence now when I tap into my intuition. I can also get a fuzzy head. I can feel hot and also mirror the feelings of the person I am coaching.

A few weeks later, I was asked to create an online course about speaking your truth and then later that week a company approached me to ask me to be a contributor of a book they were publishing. All my physical manifestations were beginning to build momentum and the work I had devotedly delivered in the past 5 years since launching my first online business were being honoured.

I was rising!

As I was willing to be seen, fellow women were seeing me. Connecting and contacting me. Then one day an exchange occurred in the radio community which meant I had to show up even stronger. It was time to write the book that I had been talking about for the past 3 years.

Meeting the writer within

An explosion of synchronicity is the only way I can describe my post lockdown life. The connections of my soul tribe, combusting into unique star constellations, waiting hungrily to light up the night sky. I believe and trust what happened next with all my heart.

What still amazes me and makes me smile is the cosmic ease of it all! Wink! Wink!

When I came up with the name Cosmic Soul School in January 2019, I was sitting super chilled at a bar in Bali. Many names presented themselves to me. But Cosmic Soul School jumped out.

Pick me! Pick me! I am the one!

It is only now with 2020 soon to be behind us that I realise the potency of the name of my business. 2020 has been the key to opening my Akasha, the soul contract written only for me. And as I remembered who I am in the unearthing of my truth, in the unfolding of this year, I unlocked a synchronicity of soul plan events.

Saying yes to Wellbeing Radio led me to be a part of the Wellbeing family WhatsApp group. In here I made connections with other incredible souls and this led me to meet with Nicola Humber who saw the light in me. As a 40th birthday gift to myself, I signed up to Nicola's mentorship.

And in 2021 Nicola, Unbound Press and I will birth my first book into the world.

As part of this divine plan, I am also being guided to glow daily and have launched my own online academy full of resources on how to Let Your Soul Fuel the Way, host my own podcast, and run a monthly Instagram TV series entitled, 'Wise Women Chats' and become a contributor for a new online lifestyle platform called mylyslife.com (Love Your Self).

So darling one, that was my 2020. Whatever it had in store for you I invite you to trust that it was right. And as you read through this book and are introduced to fellow women of light, I wish you luck as we embrace you and each other and share the beauty and power of unbound, unconditional love.

Still not sure?

As we move into 2021 and having worked with Nicola and my Unbound Sisters, I can say in the most compelling way that I don't care if you don't get me.

I do care though that you trust.

Trust! As the world is not ever what it seems. You will find your way. And if you get lost and need to find the light…

Look into my eyes

And you will see

I am Light

A force of nature

You are attracted to me

To radiate like me

And when the day is done

You lie on your back

And bask in the beauty of me

Remembering recalling

The light within

NATALIE FARRELL

Natalie is a soul-seeking, smoothie-loving, creatrix. At the age of 33, after spending 15 years of her life as a singer and vocal coach, she quit her job and headed to California to study yoga and find answers to questions she had about this thing called life!

She now shares these learnings as a writer, podcaster and intuitive coach, guiding women to create their own soul revolution. Her work is soft yet powerful and allows the women to realign to the deep connection of trust and switch back on their innate light wisdom as they wake up who they were born to be.

Ready to switch your light back on?
Tune into Natalie and her work at
www.cosmicsoulschool.com

SELECTED EXCERPTS FROM THE 2020 SOLO SELF-ISOLATION DIARIES
by Sue Sutherland

....

21st March

Day 3 and I've discovered this incredible functionality where I can talk to my laptop. The words magically appear on the page. It is dictation, and he is a bit of a dictator. A dictator who censors my words. He is a he because he doesn't let me say what I want to say.

23rd March

I'm at home, in my capital city flat, after escaping to the country with two friends last week. The plan was to sit out the looming and enforced restriction. A glorious retreat place with fire-burning sauna and outdoor hot tub to star-gaze in. Space, decadence and nature and yet, there was something off. I couldn't drop in or entirely relax.

In the face of all that was unfolding, the quiet, ungrateful voice within, became louder and louder. The inevitable moment of using my mouth words approached. To speak the undeniable within me. It wasn't my home. And so here I am, back in my flat.

29th March

My pronunciation needs to improve if I am to use this functionality.
The words I speak don't always appear on the page.
Punctuation is left to me and asterisks appear when I say "cunt," "fuck," and "bullshit."
The censoring dictator pulling his weight again.
I wonder if I could write a book this way.
Abandoning the full stop, comma and apostrophe except when absolutely necessary.
I'm almost certain I could.
Maybe I will.
The possibilities coming from solo self-isolation are revealing themselves.
I feel myself smiling at the prospect of not having to go out. Of not having to meet some of these ideas of what connection is supposed to be.
This could be one of the greatest moments of my lifetime.

17th April

I notice a tightening.
A warm feeling in my chest.

In light of COVID, I take this information in, in a way that is new to me.
Is that the point?
The attention that can only be accessed by looking inside.
We must slow down.
We must get cosy with what we find there.
What I find there is a fragility.
Beneath that is tenderness.
Hidden within is fear.
Then the surging pain.
A desire to scream.
To tear the fucking house down.
To break out of the bullshit capsule that limits possibility, creativity and expression.
Real expression of what it is like to be a living, breathing, feeling being.

23rd April

I know I must stay indoors.
I know there are going to be people who are out and making their own choices.
There is personal responsibility. A knowing from within.
An emergence of what I need to do for me, even if it is only to find out that I was wrong.
Iterating the process and being prepared for what is.

14th May

Part of me is grateful for not having, what many would call, significant others.

Those people we are beholden to.
Those that are dependent upon us, as we are
dependent upon them.
I spent most of my life trying to belong, and if you
could only see the smile. The wide, bright, open smile
on my face right now, and the way my belly takes that
deep breath.
That guttural breath of relief.
There is an inner peace of knowing.
A possibility that I am enough.
That I am where I need to be.

4th June

My drums have started talking to me.
They hang there on the walls with their beaters on top.
Waiting.
Ready for me to bring them back to life.
They make little noises.
They say hello, and I pick them off the wall.
The playing of the horse drum.
Rituals we need to remember.
I can see an owl in one and a cheetah in the other.
As I beat I feel the hurt.
The beat speaks to my heart and soul.
It is mine, and I am its.
They honour me with their presence, these drums.
It is a privilege to have them in my home.
To feel the reverberations run through my body.
That wash over and bring balance to my saturated cells.
Cells penetrated by unwanted energies.

With untold effects on this incredible body they
inhabit.

10th July

What am I hungry for?
I am hungry for the body, mind and heart of a giant
being.
A being with shoulders I have to reach up to touch.
Shoulders I can hang myself off.
A body that I can climb over.
One that can envelop me and make me feel small.
I need to feel the strength and stature of presence.
My personal climbing frame.
My personal protector.
One I can physically lean against.
Someone I can hide myself in.
To lie on.
To sniff, snuggle, stretch and purr with.
I want to purr.
I want to bring out my feline.
Who am I kidding?
It is not a pet.
It's a fucking wolf.
A masquerading, shapeshifting she-wolf.

I want to smell man.
There is a smell of man that I rarely get to smell these days.
Too often I smell fragrances designed for men rather
than the smell of a man.
I want to smell skin.
I want to smell a body.

22nd July

That big, dark monster is here again.
The one that holds the ugly truth.
That makes meaning in the unagreed.
The unsaid things.
The one that allows bombs to go off.
That lights fires.
That wants to burn the fucking place down.

I want to burn the places down.
I want to erase the memories.
To make it go away.
To remove all trace.
Deny the existence.
Remove the hope.
To feel less.
Avoid the reminder.
Creating an impasse.
A place of no return.

I have bridge burning in my bones.
I seek validation.
I set booby traps.
I test those around me.
I hide behind the words that are said.
My ugly truth hides behind the spoken words.
My smoke broken words.
Broken smoky diversion.

I let off bombs.
I wonder if people dive for cover.

I destroy.
I annihilate.
Can I temper the fire?
The fire that is fed by vulnerability.
My vulnerability and my expectations are like
dynamite.
The expectations I have.
They change everything.
They seem a little out of whack.
Hiding in the land of the unspoken voice.
My expectations are dirty, disgusting, needy and not fit
for human consumption.
I recognise how harsh and hard I am on myself.

Can I be in connection with all the trauma?
With the shame and uncertainty.
With so much risk.
I am 'too much' is written within me.
Scrawled deep into and onto my cells.
It is cellular.
It is inherited.
It is reinforced.

23rd July

I've realised something.
The more I share my feelings with people, the more
connected I am to them.
The more connected I am, the more expectations I
have.
The more expectations I have, the more dangerous it
becomes.

The trauma is exposed.
The sensitivity leaks out.
Defences go up.
Judgment arrives.
The destroyer wakes up
Bam.
I'm alone.
I die.
I create.
I take risks.
I invent.

There are amazing things that come from feeling alone.
I always have me when I am alone.
I always have this part that wants to explore.
That wants to discover.
That still has life.
The seeking part of me.
That seeking part of me is always alive.
Never truly giving up.
It's reliable in that sense.
My crutch.

My seeking is my gift and curse.

12th August

Letting go
What if I did let it go?
Despite of
Because of

Letting go of the blame apportioned to the wrong
people
So often it's women
The women in this dance get a heavier dose of
suspicion
Their betrayal is because of men
Almost every time
The circle of women is betrayed by a man
And the woman is complicit in this

A circle of women is betrayed by the presence of a man

When men are around, women are different
Women prioritise differently
They abandon what is nourishing

I love being around men
But not at the cost of being around women
Don't make me choose
Don't choose a man over a woman
Do you hear me?
Am I being clear enough for you?
Don't choose a man over a woman
It has been done too many times
It has to stop
The circles of women need to return
Women need women

I'm so fucking angry
Why did this get lost?
Why did this need get deprioritised?

I have opinions about groups of women
They are a certain way
They behave like this and look like that
Maybe I'm too man to be included in a women's circle
That's how I feel a lot of the time
The stories I have about women in circles makes it
more appealing to hang out with the men
It makes it more appealing to buck against the notion
that I am a woman

I am so much more than a woman
Woman is loaded
Woman is nice, compliant, pretty, passive and
mothering
Women lie to other women about their relationships
with men
That's how the trust gets broken
That's how the circle disintegrates
That's how the mistrust of women by women
continues
That's why I look for betrayal
I scan my environment before I speak my truth

I have a sloth on my back
I need to watch my back
How many women have been betrayed by another
woman?
And those betrayers, how many of those have been a
puppet to a man?
Who are you a puppet to?
Who pulls your strings?
Who do you jump for?

Who do you shrink near?
Who has their hand up your shirt?

That's why I have a sloth on my back
Holding on
My external counsel
Slowly raising their energy
Moving when I've hit on a good idea, or remembered
Sloth is moving now
I can feel the tingles down my arms
I want to move too

17th August

I'm not buying into this game anymore
I want to feel my feet on the ground and walk out on
the land
Get my hands in the dirt and stand skyclad under the
moonlight
To make fire and welcome in The Remembering
To feel my sex
To be a witch
To be a madame to my sexuality
I want to salivate
To feed and dance
To smile for the very virtue of being alive
For being right here right now
The magnificence of the moment
I want to cry with joy when I look at the people around
me
Realising I'm home
Knowing I am part of something

To pass something on that supports, drives, lives and loves

We can have this if we start telling the truth.

19th August

I just closed my eyes, and it was right there
Where my heart soul is
The wild twin
Close your eyes
Can you find it?
Can you feel it?
Can you see what your version of this looks like?

Now open your eyes
Look around you
Notice the difference
Are you pretending or waiting?
Hoping that it will magically appear
Is there a version that is out of reach?
A story that says you are asking too much
An impossible dream
So utterly selfish

Close those eyes again
Know that you can have this
Strive to have this
Make it happen
Breathe into it

I'm there
I can see it
I can smell it
This place where I want to be
Can I start going there today?

Close those eyes
Connect to it
Be there
Then open your eyes and notice the difference
The things around you
The people in your space
Are they who you want to be YOU with?
Yes?
Wonderful
I am delighted for you
No?
Okay
This is the first step
What do you see when you close your eyes?
Start naming it
Start drawing it
Start writing it down
Do something with it
Bring it outside of your mind
The present is begging for your attention
Do it
Please do it now

17th September

I'm leaving London
It feels so good to say that
To know that there is an end to this current situation
I want to wake up naturally
To go to bed without earplugs
To swim in natural water naked
Feeling my feet on the earth floor
Erasing the sound of drills and trucks and cars and
beatboxes and parties and gatherings
They penetrate my being
Apparently, they come written into the price
Hidden in the contract of city-dwelling
Disclaimer: loss of quiet
The sharp, holding in, of breath to avoid the cigarette
smoke
The rights of a business to make money over the rights
of an individual to rest their being
I don't like humans really
People are often my least favourite things
A tree or human?
A tree wins nearly every time
A dog or human?
The dog
Moongazing
Sun admiring
Rain smelling
I cherish these more than being with most humans
The relief from naming that!
It's not that I want to be on my own
I'd rather be on my own than with the wrong people

I remember lying in bed with a lover
He was asleep
I can't remember who it was
I was lying there awake
It was my bed we were lying in
And I felt so alone
This person didn't know me
This person didn't see me
I couldn't sleep in my own bed
That was the price of being in a relationship
That's when I realised I'd rather be on my own than in
the wrong relationship
I do keep falling into that trap however
The putting up with

The lover comes along and gives me glimpses of true
connection
There is tenderness
There is affection
Sometimes there's even love
There are aspects in this relationship which I have
craved and been seeking yet there are also elements
which I know to be deal-breakers
These deal-breakers have been lessons from the past
of what is not okay for me
Part of me sometimes thinks I can work with that and
it will be okay somehow
The lure of the shiny thing that I have been wanting in
a relationship takes precedent over what I already
know that I need
Often, it's something simple
And I find myself grasping

Grasping at this new, wonderful, endorphin-fuelled
experience
Dismissing silently what I know is not okay
Because we all know
We all know deep down when something is not okay
Deep down I knew I was biding my time
I believe we know
I believe we make excuses
We tolerate
We accept
We hope
Hope is my biggest blessing and curse
I hope that things will get better
I hope that they will suddenly change

6th October

I live in a barn on a farm, in a village with a telephone
box instead of a shop.

Anything could happen.

SUE SUTHERLAND

After two decades in the corporate world and trying to fit in, Sue became self-employed and embraced conscious sexuality, 5Rhythms, non-monogamy, power dynamics, consent, kink, nature-based creativity, trauma studies, the wisdom of the body, and more.

Sue created The Feel Institute and has a ferocious appetite for informed education, sharing experiences and helping people feel less alone with who they are on the inside.

Sue was the winner of The Unbound Press #2020VISION writing competition and is now writing their first book with us.

Find out more about Sue at:
https://thefeelinstitute.com/

REBIRTH

by Tonia Gaudiuso

....

Well 2020 really packed a punch and, as I write this, it's still not over. If you told me at the start of this year that I would live through a global pandemic, I would have laughed in your face. That's something that happens in the movies! Little did I know that in a couple of months the movies would make their way into real life. As I look back on the year I see I should have seen the foreshadowing in February when I went to the Unbound Writing Retreat in England at the magical New Forest National Park. We were five powerful women brought together by Nicola Humber (so six in total) to commune in sisterhood to receive the messages for our growth as writers and share our voices through the art of writing.

On one of the bright and sunny days we went out to convene with the trees in the forest. We began walking around and allowing ourselves to get swept away in the canvas of the trees. I found a tree I loved and I put my back to her with the intention of releasing the things that kept me playing small and inviting in the energy of expansion. While I was lying on the tree looking up at the sky I could see it gradually turning darker. Clouds began to form overhead giving us all a sign to come back together from our individual trees. Raindrops began to fall. It's as if the forest was baptizing us and washing away all the old conditioning that no longer served us. It was magical. I remember sticking my arms out, twirling in the rain, and receiving this gift from the forest and nature.

As we began to walk back to the hotel, the wind began to pick up and Mother Nature showed us how quickly things can change. A couple of minutes later, hail the size of gumballs fell from the sky and we were in shock and laughing at how bizarre it was. The quote, "Life is not about waiting for the storm to pass, it's about learning to dance in the rain" came to mind and we were dancing in the hail, till it started pelting us in the face, and it hurt. So we walked with a little more pep in our step and throughout it all laughing out loud at the fury of Mother Nature and how quickly she changes moods and does not apologize for it! This was a big lesson for me. It felt like nature was showing me how to give myself permission to be all of who I am, on the bright days and on the dark ones. It's okay to be fierce and powerful. It's okay to be all of me and she showed me how on that day, with conviction and unapologetically. Sometimes nature is pleasant and gentle (like when we left the hotel) and other times fierce and destructive (like on our walk back). It's always for a purpose, whether we are aware of it or not and she doesn't allow us to know the reason or agree to stop her because she trusts in herself and her power.

All of us felt the power of that experience and that nature showed us her destructive side for a reason. It's necessary when creating a new world – old ways must fall in order for the new ones to come in. We came together as unbound women to live in a world that's no longer under the thumb of the patriarchy. That takes conviction. We committed to leading the way for that to happen in our lives in whichever way it shows up for us, uniquely and individually. We knew together in sisterhood we were unstoppable. I don't think any of us knew that the tide had already begun to change and it was showing up in the form of a global pandemic. Mother Nature did something to us all that day, telling us to get ready for what was to come. Reminding us sometimes it has to get ugly in order for beauty to come through.

"Nature My Teacher"

I sit and embrace the beauty of nature. I allow its dynamic nature to reflect the beauty I found in me.

I stop and allow the sun to wash its warmth all over me. Soaking in its love.

I observe the birds flying joyfully and free. I allow their freedom to enter my heart.

I stop and listen to the waves of the ocean. I allow the natural flow of the water to teach me how to embrace the flow of life.

The beauty of nature is reflected in my soul.

Little did I know that stepping foot off the plane from my trip to England and a job in Ireland would be the last time I was getting on a plane for 2020, which is very rare for a traveler like me. Living in Brooklyn at one of the very first epicenters in the United States was quite crazy. The world was changing and during the three months of lockdown in New York (March, April, May) it all seemed to mesh into one very long day. What I witnessed in those months is an opportunity for a global recalibration of what really matters in life; people, our loved ones, breathing, health, touch, connection, shelter, food, being in service, being outdoors, and space. All the things, I believe have been taken for granted. This is where I began to see the silver lining in the pandemic. It was a call back to the simple things in life and to what really matters. Hugging our loved ones. Kissing people hello. Smiles to a stranger. The incredible job our teachers do with children and our youth. Seeing how important our essential workers are and the jobs they do that have been overlooked, got flipped on its head. The value of the human being. Through the chaos, I saw a message coming through. Destruction for construction.

On May 25th, the chaos heightened with the murder of George Floyd, exposing more grief and injustice that the African American community has been enduring for hundreds of years. So much grief. So much death. A reminder that human decency is still being thrown out the window. For the African American community this was nothing new, just more disappointment in our nation turning a blind eye to racism and inequality. It was hard to face the truth that as a white woman I was one of them. I was unaware and didn't know the numerous names of African Americans who had died unjustly, in the hands of those meant to protect us. My parents didn't have to have 'the talk' with me about what to do if I was ever pulled over by the police. I didn't have to worry about not getting a job before ever even opening my mouth because I was being judged by the color of my skin. The list goes on and on. I didn't know because it didn't impact my white world. Because I didn't make it my responsibility to educate myself in such things and learn the truth of racism and what is going on in the world I live in. That's what privilege does – protects me from having to deal with the discomfort of inequality.

I was ashamed that I had allowed my privilege to protect me for this long. I made sure I watched the video of George Floyd being murdered so I could feel the rage, sadness, shock, and heartbreak that I normally avoid feeling because it's too hard to see. It clicked – me choosing to be silent has me as a part of the problem. Racism is not a problem for the African American community to fix because it impacts them (shaking my head at the ignorance of this statement). It's white people's responsibility to wake up to their privilege and no longer stand for it. For a long time I was complacent to it. I didn't think I was a racist because I wasn't going around saying inappropriate things or excluding people because of the way they looked. Therefore, I thought I wasn't a part of the problem. I'm off the hook. When I checked myself, I saw the times I've tried to protect my privilege.

I justified racism not being my problem because it didn't involve me. I wasn't a part of "those" white people who are racist – as if they can be separate from who I am, trying to protect my white fragility. My family lineage isn't those of slave owners. In fact, they are immigrants who came over from Italy, poor, and had to make their own way in the world. They suffered discrimination for being immigrants when they came into this country, so I'm not a part of the problem. I didn't participate in racism. I didn't want to own that being white and being born in America meant taking responsibility for learning the truth of what this country is built from – its slaves and the poor. It's the land of the free with an asterisk. The asterisk represents anyone who is not a white, privileged man. George Floyd woke me up to my ignorance and I felt ashamed for being blind for so long. Choosing my comfort over linking arms with my African American brother and sisters, and all people who suffer from racism, injustice, and inequality. No longer would I choose safety over injustice and I'm sorry it took this long.

I'd use my white privilege to be part of the solution and use my voice to speak out against it and to educate myself on the history of the African American community from their perspective. I'd use empathy and listen to the stories. I'd speak out when I see those in my white world unaware of their privilege. 2020 kept doing its thing and unveiling all the illusions of the structures and systems meant to be in place for the people, but are not. They are for some, not for all. Having a president who promoted racism and division just made the false truths our country was built on become apparent. The patriarchy clearly still exists and is actively at work. The truth that I saw and held onto is that the shit has to come to the surface in order for it to be swept clean. You can't clean a cupboard till you know what's in it. 2020 was clearly showing us all the dirt in our nation's cupboard. All I can think is, 'It's time to get sweeping!'

I was going to end my story here but while writing this piece I found out a family member in Italy passed away, my Zia Franca, my grandmother's sister. I just came home with my mother from telling my 94 year old Nonna that her younger sister, 87, passed away in Italy. I recognize me justifying her death with how many years my aunt has been on this planet but it doesn't remove the feeling of loss, longing and sadness. The pain of losing a loved one does not discriminate by age. A piece of our family puzzle was physically gone and every year since 2018, me and my family have experienced the death of a significant loved one, getting all too familiar with the experience of it, but seeing it differently each time. In twenty nineteen with my uncle's death I was able to experience beauty in death. With all the death we are experiencing this year, I thought this was important to share.

I learned death offers us an opportunity for a new relationship to get formed with the person we lost, one from our memories. They live within our hearts, minds and the stories we tell. Death is a transition, the physical form gone but the emotional remains. The love, the laughter, the memories still keeping this family member alive. When we experience the loss of a loved one it hurts so bad. It's heartache but also an opportunity for the heart to crack open and for there to be an outpouring of love, if we allow ourselves to go through all the emotions of it. The sadness, anger, rage, grief, loss, tears, the longing, the memories and the laughter. The pain is a result of all the love experienced and shared with that person. There's something beautiful in knowing that. It means we loved deeply in our lives. Moments of joy start to come through the grief and a knowing that the sorrow is because a deep profound love was experienced. Even though the physical form of that person is no longer present, the love remains. That experience of love and those memories are something no-one can take away from us. The whole world is experiencing grief right now, hearts cracking open all over the place. I wonder if this loss of loved ones will allow for transformation and something new to come through? I know it has for me. That's what death does if you allow it. It offers the gift of a rebirth. Yet again another lesson we can learn from nature, death and rebirth. I sit and wonder, 2020 what will your rebirth be?

That's the power of chaos. It shows us what's not working. Chaos is the calling for clarity and it paves the way for it. 2020 was a year of pure chaos. Shaking everything up and showing us what's not working. That's the only way to rebuild, by knowing what didn't work. I believe since the loss has been so tremendous, there's a grand opportunity for real change and calling back to simplicity. Systems that serve the people and leaders who serve from a place of compassion and love. An intention of unity and oneness where we all thrive. Color, race all get blurred together. We respect and celebrate our differences knowing that underneath it all we all have a heart that beats and blood running through our veins. May we, from the chaos, start building a new world of love, kindness, equality, justice, community, prosperity and abundance.

TONIA GAUDIUSO

Tonia Gaudiuso is the author of The New Commodities. She is a money expert, supporting individuals and small businesses, who loves to guide her clients as they turn their money pain into a life full of joy and freedom.

She believes we are each born unique, with our own special gifts. Ever since she was a little girl, she knew her superpower was money management and organization. Hell, her favorite childhood toy was a cash register and she has been working in finance for over two decades.

Her close friends call her the money whisperer. She understands the emotional blocks and life-long habits that people inherit around finance and is in tune with what people need to clear in order to have a healthy relationship with their money.

Find out more about Tonia and her work at **www.toniag.com**

2020 - A YEAR OF DUALITY
by Tara Jackson

....

At the beginning of 2020, my long term relationship was ending. We decided to part ways, and I had booked a flight at the end of February to spend a couple of months at my childhood home back in Kenya, leaving the flat I was in with my partner, and the life I had built in London for the past 20 years.

I put all my belongings in storage, knowing that when I returned I no longer wanted to live in London. I was ready for a change, and my body, mind and soul had been craving nature and open spaces for a good few years now.

As I got back to Kenya, my parents were taking advantage of the fact that I'd be there with my youngest brother (and his carers) who has many special needs, and were going to France and the UK for a few weeks to spend time with my step-mother's sick father.

But, just 10 days later the world went into lockdown, my parents got stuck in France and I was in Kenya with my brother.

What came from the months that followed, was a rising of many things I'd still not dealt with – the shadow, parts of me I'd forgotten or ignored, triggers that I still felt. It was like 2020 was asking for it all to surface. But, this time when they did, I realised the strength, resilience and tools I had to support myself. Although there were some dark times, there was so much opportunity to be had in each of them. Looking back at it now, I see how I experienced such contrasts, how I was given one side of the pendulum to become aware of the other. This was a year of duality for me.

Loneliness leading to connection

I felt extreme loneliness rise up. I had many nights where I woke up feeling so alone, desperate and empty. It reminded me of when I first left Kenya to go to University in London. I was so homesick, and saying I hated it, would be putting it mildly. Now in the exact opposite situation 20 years later, I was homesick for my life in London.

This time, I did something I'd only kind of done before – I asked for help from the non-physical – from the Universe, the Divine, from my mother who passed away when I was eight (who I have been feeling more and more connected to), from the forest beings I felt in the garden and from my dragons I'd started connecting with recently.

I have felt so much connection with my non-physical support team, I no longer feel alone. Don't get me wrong, I also crave human connection in the physical, but having the non-physical to lean on this year, is something that got me through some dark nights when I woke up at 3am questioning everything. As I asked for help, sometimes crying out loud in despair, I felt waves of love wash over me. I surrendered to all that I was feeling, letting it come out and I felt myself truly held by something bigger than me, with a deep knowing that it will all be okay.

From feeling I had no direction to finding my niche

At the start of 2020, I felt like I had no idea what I was doing with my business. I had been in a space of seeming nothingness for almost six months. Whenever I connected with my intuition, asking for guidance on my next step, I wouldn't receive anything. One time I felt a giant cocoon, as if what was coming was still metamorphosing. I felt that something would come, I just didn't know when.

It did.

In less than an hour at the end of January the idea for a business to support empath entrepreneurs online (linking each of the seven main chakras in the body to a different part of your business) flooded out of me and combined all of my experiences and areas I'd worked in for the past 20 years.

It was such a magical experience and truly taught me the importance of trusting and allowing the process. Today, I am continuing to grow this business so smoothly and with joy, following the breadcrumbs of intuitive guidance as they are given to me. Through this work I have also connected with people and made more magical connections than I have in the past 4-5 years of having my own business, and feel like I have found my niche.

Feeling trapped, to finding creative freedom and journeying beyond my wildest dreams

In a year with so much restriction on travel and general moving around – I was also in a place where I couldn't even go anywhere on my own (I don't have a driver's licence and you need one to get around in Kenya). Even though I am a bit of a self-proclaimed hermit, I too was missing the ease with which one can step out your door in London and go for a walk, just for a change of scene. Yes, I was incredibly blessed to be in a house over-looking a forest and have nature on my doorstep, but, like many globally during lockdown I also felt trapped physically.

But, as I surrendered to the situation I began to train in colour therapy, and re-visited a long held love I had for past life regressions, I found freedom, and I began to journey in different ways.

I started painting, inspired by the colours I was learning about – letting myself get lost in their hues. Exploring how each made me feel. What emotions each colour brings up and how they are a mirror to what I am feeling in that particular moment. I got lost in a magical world of far-away lands and visions, with days turning into weeks, passing by, as I dove further in.

Alongside this, the colours began to bring up links to past lives and in the evenings, lying in bed I would regress myself (sometimes with the help of audios by Dr. Brian Weiss) into memories and experiences from this and many, many other lifetimes. These journeys were great to explore triggers I was feeling and getting to the root cause, or just allowing myself to go back and trust that what came up was what I needed. I have been to Atlantis, Egypt, Ancient Greece, the US desert, India (to name a few) other planets and beyond. Even though some of the regressions were not that pleasant, there was always something in there for me and I am so grateful to have travelled in this way. I also often used these journeys as food for my artistic creation and between the two experiences a whole new world of adventure and possibility has opened up for me.

From giving to surrendering to deeper levels of receiving

After seven months of being alone at home with my brother, spending every afternoon and evening with him to give his carers a break, I was exhausted, and ready for a break. I definitely gained a new, deep-found respect for carers, as it's intense having to give all the time and be present with someone who has such unique needs.

A week after my parents got back I came down with Covid. Amazingly nobody else did. I knew I was really run down, and it hit me. I was out, mostly asleep, exhausted with body pains and fever for a week, then in bed for another two, and it took another five to six weeks of various head symptoms before I began to start feeling like me again. During this time I was looked after in a way I don't ever remember experiencing as a child. Being the eldest of seven there wasn't much time for being sick and I kind of got on with it if I did ever feel bad.

So, even though I didn't feel good there was so much I received in the surrendering to being cared for. It began with fresh home-cooked meals being brought to my door (I know how lucky I was to be where I was), being given all the supplements, herbs and essential oils, being taught breathing exercises by my stepmother in the garden at a distance, being asked how I was feeling a few times a day, getting dietary support to help with the head issues. Then as I was able to go out I received Reiki treatments, more breathwork, meditation exercises and acupuncture.

This has opened doors to an even greater level of receiving, from others, which is an area I didn't really allow myself to go into before. I thought that if I am caring for myself and giving to myself, that's all I really need. But to receive from others, to allow yourself to receive from others, openly and without guilt or expectation in return is truly transformative.

Finding greater resolve and peace within

It's interesting reflecting back on this year, which at the time of writing is not fully over yet. I also know as time goes on, more insights and 'aha' moments will come from this year. But the most significant thing I have experienced is how I feel within myself.

I started this year knowing that there would be some difficult times ahead. I knew that I would have no home for a while; a relationship ending, and I was unclear about my work. It felt like I was having another awakening, where all my structures and stability had come crashing down. Little did I know there was even more to come.

Whilst there were many WTF moments and a few 'Why is this happening to me?' ones, there was so much for me, in these times. As a coach who is all about embodiment in life and business, I know how powerful it is to dive into the body – all the feelings and emotions – as that's how I will be able to alchemise them into the treasures.

Allowing myself to feel everything as it happened: to cry, to get angry, to feel sadness, loneliness, despair even, opened doors to even greater healing and resolve from issues I was still carrying. I spent a lot of time with my inner child – in fact I spent time with many different younger versions of myself, looking after her and supporting her as I needed then.

Having the time and space this year to really go into the shadow, to really sit with everything that came up, to honour all of it and allow it to be what it is, whilst simultaneously growing and expanding, has truly been a gift for me. (I do want to acknowledge how grateful I am that I could do this, as I know many others' situations have not afforded them this).

Letting go of what I thought I wanted my life to be and going with what this year has brought me, has definitely been challenging, but I feel so much gratitude for it all and a deep sense of peace within, a knowing that it has all been perfect.

TARA JACKSON

Tara is a business intuitive and mentor, Colour Mirrors alchemist, and the founder of Empathpreneurs®, a business service for empath entrepreneurs supporting them to align and ground their businesses with the chakras.

As well as looking at the practical elements of running an online business from systems and processes to PR and marketing, done in a way to honour the needs of sensitive souls, she also supports her clients to clear and release blocks to business impact and success through ancestral and past life healing, and colour therapy.

Her recently released second book Embodied Business looks at each of the seven main chakras, with the earth star and soul star chakras as anchor points, in terms of any blocks that might come up which prevent you from showing up in each of these areas as they relate to your business.

Find out more at:
www.empathpreneurs.org

soul lemonade

by Natalie Windle Fell

....

welp, the deal that we had been working on all of 2019 was over. everything we had been breaking our backs over felt pointless. the negotiations, the deadlines, the meetings where we had to schmooze our way through to the end in the name of selling the business – just like that, it was nothing.

they told us that it was because they were moving in another direction, but we both knew it was way more than that. the guy who was supposed to be closing the deal on their end was an incompetent douchebag. my dad was way smarter than he was, and everyone knew it. it was the elephant in the room. buying my dad's business was the smartest thing that company could have done for themselves. the products we make are top of the line, our customer service is like a warm hug in a cold industry, but that's nothing without my dad's years of invaluable expertise.

i guess in the end, it was just way too much for the douchebag's ego – the thought of someone coming in from the outside and outshining him. it was so clear. crystal clear, in fact – the absolute spite. who cancels a business deal with timing like that? who cancels a business deal – over an email – after an entire year of our free consulting and trips to their offices? who fucking cuts off a business sale negotiation with an email, knowing that my dad was going to read it immediately after he walked out of his own mother's funeral? an embarrassingly lame, socially distant, limited to 10 people, poor excuse of a funeral for a woman who loved her big family more than anything? who no-one got to say goodbye to because the nursing homes all got locked down in a moment's notice?

a fucking douchebag, that's who.

....

it was the beginning of march. i was a year and a half out of my abrupt departure from my high-paying corporate job and my funds were just about tapped out. working with my dad had been my saving grace, and this business deal we were working on was our ticket, our permission to breathe out. my dad would finally get the chance to go play golf whenever he wanted to, to finally sit back and enjoy the fruits of his labor. the business he grew was going to what we thought were great hands and my dad would be able to coast into the sunset.

and for me, it meant a lump sum of money and more time bought as i fumbled through and figured out what the fuck my soul wanted me to do, because i was really really really tired of trying. tired of suffering.

i lost my shit that night, on my way to therapy. i don't know if it was the uncertainty of covid making its way through philly, the fact that my grandmom had an essentially family-less funeral, or that my finances were once again in jeopardy and i was once again googling how to declare bankruptcy. it was probably a combo of all three, coupled with the way that march in philadelphia really gets under my skin. the way it just has everyone so goddamn tired of the cold and makes you laugh like the joker the way it snows on the first day of spring.

my therapist emailed me earlier that day, saying that it might be the last time we had a face-to-face session and that she'd understand if we wanted to move to telehealth, since a lot of people were concerned. but i wasn't fucking concerned about the damn virus. i was concerned that i felt like throwing myself into oncoming traffic. and i'm only half kidding. i was showing up to that session.

the darkness that took over scared the shit out of me. i hadn't felt that way since 2012 when i was perpetually piss drunk, laying on my shitty hardwood floor, wondering who the hell i was.

i got into my car and my heart was racing. i didn't really leave myself enough time to properly find parking (i never do). i thought i hit the jackpot and pulled into a spot, only to be shooed away by a valet guy – i was in front of a brazilian steakhouse. i rolled down my window and with the glazed over, intense, fake niceness of a serial killer, i calmly said, "oh, i'm sorry," and pulled away. and then i started hysterically crying.

i'm such a failure. i can't do anything right. i'm a 34 year old fucking piece of shit nothing. i'm not successful. i'm lost. maybe everything i feel inside IS a mental disease. maybe i should just go back on medication. fuck it. numb me. someone. please.

the parking spot i found was so far away from the building my therapist was in, but i had no other choice. it was either that or drive home – i mean, i was already so late. but i was so out of my skull upset, i don't think being alone right then would have done anything but made things worse. it was so goddamn windy. i tried to put my hood up over my head as i was walking. but it kept blowing off. and i was crying hysterically, loudly. just walking down the busy center city blocks wailing, passing people who all gave me extremely concerned looks, some of them half-stopping, but not knowing what to say. i didn't even fucking care.

i finally made it and pretty much collapsed on my therapist's couch, snot pouring out of everywhere it pours out in times like that. and she held space for me as i calmed down.

and then something weird happened.

i was explaining to her about why i was so upset. being late for the session. the funeral. the business deal going sour. my finances. my life. my deep seated feelings of failure stemming from childhood contrasted with my deep seated knowing that i'm here for a reason. i let it all out, and that's when i realized that it felt like i was watching myself. the words were coming out, but were they mine? who was talking? was it really me or someone else?

it was like i was playing a witness to my own pathetic drama. and as an observer, it wasn't so pathetic. it actually made a lot of fucking sense. i left the session, able to breathe again. no problems were solved, but i didn't feel like numbing myself or wanting to jump in the river. i felt...enlightened? what the hell just happened to me? i felt like that catharsis that was expelled from me was some kind of demon. one that had been latched onto my insides with its long demon nails, leeching lifeforce from my absolute core. but now that it was out, there was this strange kind of void. what was it?

as the weeks passed after that, nothing about my situation changed at all. i continued to hemorrhage money without a plan b, continued to rack up my debt. but i just sat in it. i surrendered. the demon that fed off my frantic grasping for answers was dead now. so what else was there to do? as i watched local businesses close, watched the country go into lockdown, i accepted it. as my husband lost his job, i accepted it. i accepted the terrible struggle we had of him going through six weeks without pay because the PA government blows harder than free willy. i accepted when i found out that i had shingles on my fucking birthday. who gets shingles in a pandemic that's not shingles? whatever, i sat in it. and it subsided. i sat and i sat and i sat. every time i felt like the demon was about to slide into my metaphysical DMs, i looked up at the sky and was like "tell me what i'm supposed to do here, because i'm done trying," and every time – every single time, i got the answer to just accept. just surrender.

and that's how 2020 wound up being for me – a fucked up, twisted tale of personal and collective surrender. and if you would have told me the night i had a pre-therapy straightjacket meltdown that this would be the best year of my life, i would have killed you with my bare hands.

no, i didn't win the lottery. my dad didn't sell his business. my husband's job in a restaurant is still very much in a covid-wrapped touch and go. i honestly have never been more uncertain in my life. but the lesson that the universe gave me this year is that nothing is ever certain – ever. it wasn't before now, it isn't this year, and it never ever will be – so what do you do about that? you live your fucking life regardless. you grin, and you bear it, and you laugh in the face of the old version of you who thought you could control your life and everything in it.

you press on. you throw your hands up in the air and find yourself amidst the panic. you find your voice amidst the rest of the world as they're screaming and running around like chickens with their heads cut off. you really drive home the fact that nothing outside of you defines your worth, your soul, your purpose. you feel god hugging you because you are a precious, boundless, piece of the goddamn cosmos.

no lack of money, biohazard, or government tyranny could EVER take away my trust that everything is always going to be OK and perfect, no matter how bad it looks. it really is possible to make insanely addicting soul lemonade out of some really rotten and mouldy lemon conditions. try it. you might not believe it at first, but the universe doesn't really care about you believing as long as you trust. so trust.

thanks, 2020. love you, mean it.

NATALIE WINDLE FELL

Natalie Windle Fell is the author of Rude Awakening: A Mixtape – an unconventional guide to spiritual awakening in the form of personal stories, backed by an inspirational playlist.

In 2018, Natalie quit her corporate job without a backup plan and dedicated her attention to her own awakening and helping others along the path. She loves cooking, art in all forms, and off-color humor. Natalie currently lives in Philadelphia with her husband and rambunctious Pomeranian.

Hang out with her on Instagram
@nataliewindlefell

I FEEL
by Jo Gifford

....

My 2020 vision was forged in the fire of my grieving heart and splintered soul.

The seasons meandered through the year; the budding wheat, the scorching sun, the amber leaves, the frosty, cobwebbed branches all bearing witness to my growth, my downfalls, and my emerging newness.

Nature has nestled my essence.

Gaia has opened up her earthy arms, and held me close in her muddy, pebbly bosom.

My hot tears were shed in the arms of the tree – *my* tree – that provided rooted strength, ancient wisdom, and boughs that were arms for my ache.

I questioned the lake, looking into the cool, gentle ripples at my reflection for guidance.

The rivers have become portals to the sacral freedom of my wilder self; their watery ripple a potent potion to alchemise the quantum leaps of the new me.

I discovered the soothing magic of the muddy water.

I cried in the freezing cold, salty sea.

I laughed with the joy of my inner child as the waves lapped at my edges, sluicing off the sadness, gently rubbing away fear to expose a raw expansion.

A vulnerable, newly melded me.

My feet tramping the earth of the fields behind my house, rooting in the ways I have changed.

Loss leaves you changed.

Deep grief arrives in waves. My father. My dad.

No-one we love should ever die alone. A screen shouldn't be the way you say goodbye for the last time.

While dementia took my dad like a wild, twisted, feral vine over the last two years, COVID had the final say.

While his lungs bled out, our hearts broke.

His soul went home, and the moment we knew was coming played out in a way we could never have imagined.

Nor were we prepared for the pain of grief in isolation.

No big family hugs, no extended celebrations; no messy, snotty, howling cries with my siblings, no memories shared in person.

No shared humanity.

No connection.

No touch.

No words.

Grief brought me to my knees, my human-ness cracked open, a rawness where love and guttural loss connect all of us to the experience of what it means to live.

Yet the vision of 2020 was to rise.

A purpose I could not see in the sheets of my hot tears, in the burning hot terror, despair and surrender.

I am burned, melded, renewed, rewired, reignited, reborn with a sense of power and purpose so strong, so visceral, so timely, it must have been woven in the stars.

Where struggle laid me bare, expansion gave me the tools to heal. Where humanity wore me down, power and purpose re-sourced me.

My connection to all, to myself, to my creativity, my spirit, my brilliance, and my life has been plugged into the big vision of all.

I feel my now-ness, my new-ness, my why, my power, my source.

I feel in full range.

I feel in full colour.

I feel in full acceptance.

I feel in full surrender.

I feel like myself.

I feel as myself.

I feel for us all.

I feel connected.

I feel on purpose, re-SOURCE'd, re-imagined.

I feel.

JO GIFFORD

Jo Gifford is an author, entrepreneur, and content marketer for changemakers. She believes that we create change through human connection and owning our unique brilliance.

Find out more at: **https://www.jogifford.co**

2020 – THE DEATH OF WHAT
NO LONGER SERVES
by Stephanie Starla

....

I had BIG plans! 2020 would be my year. I had turned 40 in November 2019 and I knew this year I would SHINE my light! I had a clear vision of what I was going to create, who I was going to serve and I was on a mission to realise it. However, 2020, the planets and the Universe had other plans.

My mentor, Karen Yates, often said, "Have a plan but hold it lightly," something that has got me through this year. Sadly, she left us at the beginning of 2020. As I sat at her funeral, I could feel death sit beside me, wanting to converse, but I turned away. I wasn't ready to hear what it had to say.

The following months were full-on. As the news of lockdown hit, I moved into action. 'How can I serve?' was my mantra. I turned to my group of over 800 holistic business owners and created a plan to help with this monumental pivot! From that, some amazing things happened. Collaborations flourished, online magazines, women's summits and online courses. So much came together throughout those months, along with a roller-coaster of emotions as we navigated these times of uncertainty.

All the while, the fear of death was imminent. I couldn't seem to shake it. The death toll announced every day, the news of numbers rising never far from someone's lips, even if you turned off the TV. Fears of my own mortality and those I love, haunted me. Death of businesses, relationships, friendships. Wherever I looked, I faced death and it took its toll.

Instead of holding space for this natural part of the cycle – I ran, I numbed. 'Busy' was my drug of choice. While I watched many take this time to slow down, I quickened my pace, taking on more and more so I didn't have time to converse with Death.

It was the nights that were the hardest – the time where I let the fear overcome me. I went to bed most nights unsure if I would wake in the morning. I knew death was coming; I didn't know who or what it wanted.

It was just before Samhain; a blue moon was on the horizon to shed more light on the thinning veils and my birthday was approaching. The irritation of what no longer served me was prickling my skin like an itchy jumper. I wanted to shrug it off, cast it aside, but no matter how much I tried, I was stuck with it.

Often I wondered what was death coming for? Was it one of my loved ones? Was it my own life? Did it want to cast its decay on my business or friendships? I knew without a shadow of a doubt that the end of something was nigh, and yet no real clarity of what that would be.

Then it happened. I broke. My health and mindset spiralled and I found myself lying on the floor unable to breathe – it was my time. My time to face death.

I remember the night the ambulance was called. So close to passing out, fear gripped my chest tight. There was nowhere to run.

As I sat waiting for the delayed medics, a sense of peace came over me. Clarity came and I saw, it wasn't the end of me or my life on this planet. The vice-like grip on my heart was not a physical one; it was an emotional one. Once again, death came to sit beside me and I turned to face it. Tears falling from my eyes as I knew an ending was on its way. The only thing to do was surrender.

For days I rested. Hit pause on my life as I awaited the news from Death. What it finally delivered shocked me. It wasn't the end of my mortality – it was the end of my marriage.

Nearly 20 years of marriage, 25 in total together, was to end. He was my childhood sweetheart, the father to our three children, my best friend and lover. I heard him say the words, "I think we should separate," and I knew that this was the grip of Death.

In hindsight, it probably shouldn't have come as a shock. In my heart and soul, I knew that a 'traditional marriage' wasn't for me. I had felt like a caged bird for so long. But I loved him, and I knew he loved me. Yes, there were issues, but the romantic in me believed we could overcome anything, even though with each year my health deteriorated and joy was often missing.

I knew neither of us could hold on to a dream that meant compromising our happiness for the sake of being together. How that awareness hurt!

I left our family house and fell into the arms of my soul sisters, who held me while I crumbled.

I knew that I couldn't return. After 14 years of living in a house that never felt like home, it was time to move forward, the direction was unknown but the need was Divine. All the dreams that I had shared for my relationship diminished. The plans for my life went up in flames. I stared into the future I had so much belief in and watched it all dissipate.

At that moment I saw Father Time standing beside Death – in astrology, we had been blessed with Saturn conjunct Pluto – The Father standing beside the Great Destroyer – and I knew they had been tailing me since their coming together in January. It was my time to face their teachings.

I could feel my heartbreak and I prayed to the Goddess to lead me. I started to feel a stirring. A flicker of hope as a new life was being forged in the fires of hell. The Goddess showed me that I would rise from the flames more powerful than ever before. I knew this death was going to be the most painful I had ever experienced and yet, I trusted through my surrender to Her.

I found myself called to a holiday cottage near a Scottish loch to spend time there with my children. It is truly the most magickal of places that has been my healing balm. I can feel my roots begin to unfurl from the pot that was far too small and grow deep into the earth below my feet. Her waters heal me. Her land nourishes me and the air breathes new life into the possibility of happiness.

A new life is emerging and while I still grieve for the death of the old one, I know, without a shadow of a doubt that the excitement of what could be, will spark the flame to begin again. The old wounds of the past seem to have been ripped open this year and although I feel battered and bruised, I trust that the healing process has begun.

As I write this now, having just turned 41 and 2020 is coming to a close, all my plans for this year in my new decade are shredded and I find myself without a husband, home or family close by. My business is up in the air; the only consistent thing is this; the words that flow on the page.

To some, this may look like a disaster, but to this Scorpio Sun woman, this is what I was born to do – rise like the Phoenix from the ashes of old to transcend into flight once more.

2020 has shown me that death comes in many forms; there is no running or hiding from it. Facing it head-on in the dark nights of the soul is the only way to dance through 'til dawn. What is inevitable is dawn will always come, with it the promise of new beginnings.

We as a society have learnt to fear death or the season of Winter. However, without it, we would not know Spring, Summer or Autumn. Winter is a necessary part of life, a time of decay, stillness, surrender, death and root deep nourishment. Trust you have all the magick of the seasons within and you will have the fullness of life running through you once more.

If you ever forget that, fear not, just look out of your window – Mother Nature shows us the way.

2020 thank you. Thank you for your teachings, your lessons and blessings. What once was is no more. We are in the natural cycle of things and this new decade has shown us that change is inevitable. The truth is, acceptance, surrender and love will help us through.

We all get these gifts from life and it is important to remember that this my friend, is METAMORPHOSIS – the key to your inner transformation so you too can feel the power of life, death and BE-ing a human that changes, evolves and grows. I believe the power is within us all to embrace so we can create the lives we love.

It's Our Time!

STEPHANIE STARLA

Stephanie Starla is a Women's Empowerment Coach and Passion Priestess living in the heart of Scotland. She is dedicated to helping women unleash their sacred, feminine power and to help them create a life they LOVE.

Stephanie is revolutionizing business by teaching women how to awaken their own inner Priestess to build a business that GETS RESULTS while aligning to their SOUL PURPOSE! She has an array of online and in-person workshops and coaching, delivered in a down to earth, holistic way that help women to flourish in all areas of their lives!

https://stephaniestarla.com/

FULL CIRCLE
by Lucy Anne Chard

....

I place my bones on the riverbank, and shed the last layer of my skin. The wound where my heart used to be is a punctured place,

filled with stale blood and things left unsaid,

I cannot breathe.

I'm becoming a creature of the Underworld.

Transparent and raw, like a pupa,

I wait.

Shimmer on the water; a sea spray in the air.

A lightning sprite across the African sky…

Ah yes!

That's where it went.

The other part of me that used to be,

I remember.

Slowly, I'm rebuilding my voice,

with the rustle of the birds, and the humming of the trees.

New bones forming with the mud from the riverbank,

heavy with minerals, and aeons of ancestry.

This Underworld me is stronger,

softer, more open.

Fortified with Time, and Memory, and Silt.

Ready to be reborn, now of a different sort.

Loved ones gone before carry me home with the river,

I am whole again.

....

I wanted to write a piece about 2020 that was upbeat – jolly even. But the words that came out just felt clammy, and lifeless.

So instead I'm going to show up raw, and be real with you. That means these words won't be even remotely jolly, but they will be vulnerable, and perhaps more importantly, honest.

My hope is this piece will offer solace to anyone who isn't ready to reframe the loss of a loved one yet, or indeed the loss of a part of themselves that they miss deeply, and that has long been buried.

My intention is that these words act as a companion piece to encourage you to simply be with yourself through the muck of it all, and know that how you feel is valid, even if you only have enough energy right now to get through one day at a time.

So this is where we begin, regardless of how loudly my inner critic shouts at me to, *"Stop being self-indulgent!"*

There's a global pandemic in 2020, and I'm an orphan at 40.

....

Like many of you, I had plans at the start of 2020.

Those plans changed dramatically when a visit to South Africa to see my Dad took an unexpected turn.

What seemed like a regular overnight stay in hospital to observe a swelling on his leg, turned into the blur of the intensive cardiac care unit, 6am phone calls from worried nurses, and a deep, deep sense of uncertainty.

After four days of back and forth hospital visits to see him, all the while hoping he'd miraculously wake up one morning feeling a whole lot better, at 2:30pm on March 5th 2020, my dear Dad died.

It takes my breath away that a whole, entire person – with full spirit, and personality, and undeniable presence – can be here one moment, and gone the next.

Dad had been in late stage kidney failure for 9 months. He was on dialysis every second day, and along with his loss of mobility – which is a common side-effect of kidney failure – he'd also been suffering with debilitating pain from unhealed necrotic ulcers on his legs. He was by no means well, but I guess my naivety, mixed with a heavy dose of denial, meant I'd struggled over the past 9 months to come to terms with the reality of my Dad being this way, and as a result I felt utterly unprepared for his death.

Nicky, the fiercely compassionate, kind and superbly efficient cardiac nurse who cared for him in those four short days, said he woke up in the morning on March 5th, ate his breakfast, and then decisively announced, *"Right, I'm leaving today."*

It was his heart that went first, in the end.

My sisters and I arrived at his bedside 15 minutes late.

....

A week after Dad's passing, I turned 40. My aunt made me a cake, and we had a small, quiet meal together as a family before the funeral the next day. Having lost my Mom in 2015, all I kept thinking about was that I never imagined I'd have buried both my parents by the age of 40.

"What about all the children who've lost their parents before they're even old enough to go to school? Stop feeling so sorry for yourself!" my internal Pity-Party

Monitor hissed at me from the Judgement seat in the back of my mind.

I calmly told her to *fuck off*.

When I returned to the UK on the last flight out of South Africa before both countries went into lockdown, I landed in a new 2020 reality.

"It's a nightmare here, you're going to struggle just to find toilet paper," the taxi driver muttered on the journey home from the airport.

As the days and weeks went by, it seemed all anyone could talk about was Covid-19, and the lockdown, and the panic buying, and the social distancing, and the hand washing, and the furloughs...and all I wanted to do was stop everything and scream, *"Just-shut-the-fuck-up-and-don't-you-know-my-Dad-died!?"* because to be candid here, it felt like there was a massive change in my 2020 reality that had nothing to do with Covid-19, and everything to do with a gaping hole that I wasn't ready to accept.

I'm sure I'm not alone in feeling that if Covid-19 was a character in a play, it'd be the overbearing, inappropriately intrusive relative who hijacks everybody's grieving process and makes it all about them.

....

I'm ashamed of how selfish that sounds.

Especially in the midst of a world that is in such a state of flux.

There's something to be said for the painful, clumsy vulnerability that comes with not knowing how to process grief in the midst of a pandemic. At times it's felt impossibly difficult to navigate graciously. I'm confident that I have no idea what I'm doing when it comes to processing grief in the 2020 landscape.

Just writing that helps take the pressure off feeling the need to reframe how I feel into some sort of bloated, half-decomposed meme.

What a relief, to simply allow all parts of me to be openly expressed, without feeling the impulse to brace myself for the well-meaning, but empty pseudo-spiritual platitudes so often regurgitated to fill the void of awkwardness that inevitably arises when other people don't know how to act around the bereaved, and are terrified that you're a super-spreader, and they too, might catch grief.

....

When Mom died unexpectedly in 2015, I couldn't stop crying. I wept on the Underground. I sobbed in the grocery store. I wrote reams of notes about the shock of her loss in my journal.

This time in 2020 it was different.

There was no weeping, no sobbing, and no writing.

Only numbness.

Days and weeks went by with no emotion. Sometimes I'd sit quietly by myself and try to cry, but all that came out was a thin, hollow sound that made my chest hurt.

So instead, I stayed busy. To fill the punctured place where my heart was.

Make a podcast. Launch a YouTube channel. Create courses. Teach courses. Show up, smile, everything is OK.

Grief, I've learned, has many different guises that you cannot anticipate, or rush your way through.

....

Along with a sense of upheaval and uncertainty this year, there's also been a powerful undercurrent of tenderness, solace, and grace. Certainly there have been moments of gentleness and heart-opening kindness that I cannot not reflect on.

I'm floored when I think about the sheer elegance of timing that allowed me to spend four days with my Dad while he was in hospital, where I got to hug him and hold his hand.

The kindness and generosity of my neighbour and friend, Amy, who stepped in without question to take care of the cats when my husband, Craig rushed onto a last minute flight out to be with me for the funeral.

My aunt and uncle, who supported me with strength and gentleness as my sisters, and Craig and I packed up Dad's house, and had those uncomfortable but necessary conversations with estate agents, probate officials, and funeral directors.

And Craig, who held me while I fell to pieces, and loved me anyway despite the cracks.

The day my Dad passed, my sisters and I came home from the hospital in the evening and sat in silence on the wooden deck in the garden of our family home, watching the sunset kiss the muddy banks of the Kromme river where Dad had loved to sail his boat, and where he and Mom had met by chance as teenagers, all those years ago in the 60s.

In that milky twilight space – when the sun dips down just below the horizon and all the creatures of the river fall silent – we were greeted by the softest rustling of giant wings, as a rare African Spotted Eagle Owl pierced the night with a haunting cry, and landed a few feet away on a branch of the tree that Dad and Mom had planted together a few years prior.

Now, I want you to know that I'm sceptical about what happens after we die. My own belief is not yet firm, hovering somewhere in-between the realms of the mystical and the realism of science.

Yet that night, seeing the Eagle Owl so free, and wild, and powerfully alive, I felt comforted. My feeling of anguish met with another feeling of quiet peace, brought on by the thought that life continues on in a strange, beautiful momentum that I don't fully understand. Perhaps the conclusion of one form just leads to the next.

Not gone, just *different*.

The exquisite, unknowable grace of it all.

....

2020 has taught me that Death is our greatest teacher about Life.

We don't just mourn the physical death of loved ones, we mourn dreams that lose momentum, and ways of being that get buried under rules, and restrictions, and "new normals," too. We mourn the endings of relationships, careers, parts of our identity that fall away, and friendships that fade over time.

Death of any sort, can feel soul-crushing and heart-breaking. In our modern society that seems to have a process for everything – including grief – I want to tell you that it's absolutely normal to feel knocked down by the loss of someone or something, or indeed, the loss of a part of you that once was.

You haven't fallen through the cracks if the processes don't work.

You're in what I've come to know as the Underworld, and the Underworld operates on its *own Time*.

My Dad was a Scientist, with a deep love and reverence for the Natural world. There's one scientific law that he held in the highest regard his whole life, that I was reminded of that evening with the Eagle Owl, and I want to share it with you:

"Energy cannot be created, or destroyed.
It only changes form."

2020 has taught me that life itself is in a constant state of reinvention, one way or another. We're all in a perpetual process of shedding one layer, growing the next, and on and on.

In 2020, I fully surrendered to the Underworld.

I let it unpeel my layers and consume me, and I emerged from it a different sort. Softer; more gentle. Accepting of my own magnificent paradoxes.

If there's something I'm going to take with me from 2020 into 2021 it's this:

However many times the wheel turns...however many times you, or I, find ourselves surrendering to the mud of the Underworld for the next phase of reinvention, and the next; we cannot be destroyed.

Only changed.

LUCY ANNE CHARD

Lucy Anne Chard is a certified clinical hypnotherapist, energy healer and transformational coach, helping sensitive rebels and creative visionaries feel seen, heard, and appreciated for who they truly are. With a background in theatre arts, television broadcasting, and human behaviour studies, she left her corporate job in 2016 to teach and guide others on how to navigate personal and professional reinvention, and live a more creatively fulfilling life.

Having studied Astrology since she was 13, Lucy regularly incorporates astrological insights into her courses and sessions with clients, as well as practical wisdom from the Human Design system, and the Gene Keys.

When not working, Lucy can be found co-hosting the Replenish Your Life podcast, creating cosmic sound healing meditations, going for long walks in nature, planning her next underwater scuba adventure, and watching sci-fi series with her husband and two cats.

Find out more at:
https://www.lucyannechard.com

WAKING UP IN 2020
by Cathy Skipper

....

Have you ever driven a familiar route in your car, for example the regular way to work, and when you got to the destination, you couldn't remember driving it at all? Well, that's because you were operating under the influence of a network in your brain called the Default Mode Network. This network carves out behavioral ruts in the brain from repetitive actions, such as the familiar route we have just talked about. When we go along these ruts in the brain and in the car, we can 'switch off' the brain in a sense, save energy and get to the destination without being 100% aware of the journey we took. This network keeps us in emotional, mental and behavioral ruts. 2020 forced many of us to wake up from the Default Mode Network.

This may all sound very complicated, but it is worth thinking about because many of us do, in fact, spend an enormous part of our lives in this default mode, which includes the stories we tell ourselves about ourselves, i.e. our ego or conscious sense of self. Then one day we wake up and we think, "How did I get here?" or "Is this really the life I should be living?"

We were semi-unconscious or maybe even fully unconscious as we made important decisions and took certain paths through our lives, until at one point, we realize like the proverbial fish in the water, we are completely surrounded by water (our habitual story of ourselves and the world) and we were completely unconscious that that was our default mode, i.e. that the water was even there.

This doesn't just happen on an individual level. It happens collectively, too. Whole communities, societies and countries follow the general consensus, or, like a pendulum, they get swung in a certain direction by the energy of the collective. Just like in the habitual car journey to work, they aren't fully aware of how they got there. Then one day, a large proportion of the country are in some way triggered by an event such as Covid-19 or a person such as George Floyd and ask themselves, "What happened?" Many of the members of that community don't believe it was anything they did, or that they had any power over the events. They feel they are victims of the system, like fish completely surrounded by water.

I envision the year 2020 as being an exceptional and vitally important year for us as individuals and as a global community. This doesn't mean that I see it as an easy year—far from it. Yet, I do see it as a gift. A gift to break the spell the Default Mode has cast over us, so we can become more conscious of our lives individually and collectively.

We were all going along an unconscious path. The societies and communities we were living in and the way we were working, surviving or even thriving were, to a large extent, never questioned. This was the way life was and that was that. Until suddenly last spring that all changed. Remember what Hunter S. Thompson said: *'When the going gets weird, the weird go pro.'*

Lockdown, fear of death, fear of the other, face coverings, job losses, conspiracy theories, quarantine, isolation, death tolls, loss of normality, profound change and unpredictable transformation are just some of the themes that the Covid-19 virus triggered in our homes and on the world stage. You could say 2020 is more than weird, it is tough, and my reply to that would be "When the going gets tough, the tough go pro."

So, what does it mean to be weird and tough enough to 'go pro'? To me, our modern society often views someone as weird when they are being true to themselves. When being authentic is not honored as essential and is even denigrated if it goes against the ideas and values of the system, you have to be tough to stay true to yourself.

For those of us who have been striving for self-realization and living our personal myth, being weird and tough may be commonplace and having the world blown apart by Covid-19 has brought us out of the woodwork and invited us to go pro. Over the years, I have become weird and tough and I own it with every cell of my body.

As the existing signposts of what was once considered normal society crumble, our skills in navigating the unconscious realms and our weirdness have become the number one survival strategies. We are now the pros in a world that has lost its compass!!

It goes deeper than this. I really believe in Marie-Louis Von Franz's suggestion that, *'The wounded healer is THE archetype of the Self.'* The guiding light of an authentic life is not a society that puts money and power at the helm, but our own unconscious that leads us deep into the hidden parts of ourselves and that shows us the layers that need peeling away so we can get nearer to our essence. These layers are the scar tissue that we have built over lifetimes to survive, to protect us from traumas, to cover our wounds.

Those who take the path of peeling away these layers must feel the traumas and the wounds that made those layers in the first place. The feeling is the portal. "To feel is to heal." In the same way as it hurts when we peel a band aid off a skin wound, we are invited to feel the repressed and buried emotions as we peel off the layers that kept us from feeling our pain—This is the path of the Wounded Healer.

2020 has snapped us out of our Default Mode Networks. The invitation is to heal and change the perspective from being stuck in the ruts of unconscious behaviors to a deep relationship with our Self, which becomes the new torch bearer. I don't believe we will ever be 'getting back to business as usual' after Covid-19.

By changing our perspective from looking outwards to becoming highly skilled navigators of the inner experience, we can imagine a world that resonates with a collective healing vibration. This collective vibration comes from each person's individual, committed, authentic inner healing journey. Like stars in the sky, we are each one of us individually responsible for bringing our healing energy and brightness to the world.

We do this by showing up from a vulnerable yet real place within. As we each shine with our own light, don't forget the wound is the place where the light gets in. We will begin to realize that our strength is not in power over others but in the vulnerability of knowing we are wounded.

The gift in Covid-19, I believe, is that nature has surpassed all man-made and natural boundaries and limits to show us that humans' behavior is pushing her out of balance. It is her nature to do whatever is needed to restore her balance. She is being gentle with Covid-19—she is giving us a warning. And, as with the psyche, when we get a message, we need to listen to it, whether we like it or not. Otherwise the message will get stronger and stronger until we do get it or until it is too late for us.

2020 didn't stop at Covid-19. It brought a shocking reality out of the collective shadow and into the light when the world heard George Floyd calling out for mama whilst he was being slowly suffocated by the pressure of a police officer's knee on his throat. I felt his call was not just to his mama, not just to all the mamas alive in the world today, not just to all the mamas in his ancestral mother-line, but to the energy of Mother Earth herself that was slowly being squeezed out of him.

He called out for life, for the life that was being forcibly taken from him and from the Great Mother. This is a huge symbol that resonated throughout the world and one that we all felt, like it or not, deep within our bodies. In one way or another, the patriarchy that we all have internalized is slowly suffocating us, squeezing the last breaths of our connection to the Great Mother out of us. People of color are on the front line. They know it is happening.

What is even more frightening to me, is that many of the privileged white community of the world are not aware that it has been happening to them, too. Knowing this lies deep within their shadows. They, too, are caught in a system that 2020 has dragged out of the unconscious and placed on center stage. We must all search inwards and find the cop within that wants to suffocate our deep connection to ourselves, to nature and to life. This is anti-life. We are not only killing black men on the streets, we are killing the indigenous human that resides in all of us.

2020 has seen an explosion in people searching to connect with their ancestors. Beholding our ancestors and honoring their journeys is a huge part of what it means to be human. By neglecting them, we are dehumanizing ourselves. A revolutionary research article written in 1987 by Cam, Stoneking and Wilson claimed to have identified the maternal ancestor of all living humans. This paper caused some reaction in the scientific world due to the fact that humanity's common ancestor was not only a woman but a black woman. To me, George Floyd's cry resonated in the present, the future and back in time to the mother of us all.

I believe, it is our ancestral grandmothers that are calling us in 2020. We must hear their cries. We need their experience and understanding. We are nothing without the accumulated wisdom of the generations of mothers that went before us. In 2020, the feminine is rising. Yet, I believe it is not enough to banter these words without deeply knowing within what these words mean. My journey of disconnection from my ancestral mothers to reconnection saved my life. Their voice is coming through in the book I am writing this year. We need the wisdom of those that came before us to flow through our beings, to parent us to support and guide us. The wisdom of the ancients is our birthright and yet we have squandered, ignored and belittled it. This is because the feminine is the keeper of our ancestral knowledge. It is not cerebral, it's visceral. It comes not through the mind, but through the body in the mitochondrial DNA. We must feel it, not think it. The feminine is rising through the mother-line. The grandmothers are asking to be heard. Let's not allow George Floyd's cry to be in vain!

The 2020 elections in America revealed a divided country and a President that refused to accept the reality that he'd lost the game. The world looked on as America's shadow was exposed through the lies, narcissism, racism, sexism and most of all gangster approach of a man that without knowing it was possessed by an archetype of the collective psyche for us all to see. The shadow is powerful when it remains unconscious. However, when a shadow element of ourselves or a country is exposed for all to see, it loses its power and deflates like a balloon.

It's not the politics or even the revealed shadow of America that interests me in 2020. It is the powerful archetype that is rising out of the ashes that I put my hope in, which gets me back to the wounded healer being THE archetype of the Self. A good friend who is an astrologer rang me up a couple of days after the election to tell me she had looked at Joe Biden's chart and he has Chiron in Aries in the 10th house, which suggests he is a leader and a wounded healer. I began to read about Biden's life. I am not a great political buff, but what interests me are the energies circulating in the collective. What I found in my research is that Biden's wound is his superpower. In addition to being constantly bullied as a child due to a stutter, in 1972, he lost his wife and baby daughter in a car accident. In 2015, one of his two remaining sons died of brain cancer. His grief and journey through it are at the heart of who he is as a person—a wounded healer.

Enantiodromia is a concept described by Carl Jung as *'the emergence of the unconscious opposite in the course of time.'* It usually happens when there is imbalance. When something dominates in the natural world, enantiodromia functions to bring equilibrium back. It rises from the unconscious. So, we rarely see it happening until it is there in front of us for all to see.

In 2020, this enantiodromia is playing out in the appearance of Covid-19 forcing us to retreat inwards in a modern world that functioned through exteriorization and looking outwards. In the widespread cry of Black Lives Matter bringing racism and white privilege to the forefront after centuries of systemic inequality. In the underlying life experiences of the new President of the United States, whose journey through grief and healing cannot but influence his role as a leader, in comparison to the spoilt, narcissistic, gangster-like qualities we have been confronted with lately. 2020 has taught me that we are all connected. The planet is small. The personal cannot be separated from the collective. The journey inwards is more important than anything. Our inner lives mirror and reflect the outside world. The unconscious is far wiser than the ego. The ancestors are calling us.

2020 has taught me that to be human is to feel—to feel our pain, our joy, a sense of belonging, our creativity, our responsibility to the whole. Isn't this what the angels are jealous of us for?

CATHY SKIPPER

In 2015, over a period of 6 months, Cathy lost her mum, met her soul partner, moved continents, was diagnosed with cancer, had her ten-year old son hijacked by his father, and lost every material possession she owned. This huge life change felt like a death. The old Cathy was dying and she was in a gateway, where she could die of cancer or if she survived, be reborn.

With the help of aromas, journaling, affirmations, Jungian depth psychology, psychedelics, a twin flame relationship, the desert…Cathy navigated the journey to healing and rebirth. It was a question of life or death.

All her work is based on her own journey as a wounded healer. She is totally familiar with navigating the unconscious realms, the ancestral realms, the plant and animal realms. She coaches and teaches from a place of experience.

Find out more at: **aromagnosis.com**

2020 WAS GOING TO BE MY YEAR
by Sarah Weale

....

2020 was going to be my year.

I know, I know… everyone says that, but truly. 2020 was going to be my year.

This year has been imprinted in my subconscious since I was a little girl. When I was six years old, a family friend asked me a series of rapid fire questions about when I might hit certain life milestones. She meant for it to be light and silly, but always the perfectionist, I got serious, contemplative. I answered as honestly as I could, from the heart.

When will you find a job? 2020.

When will you fall in love? 2020.

When will you start a family? 2020.

Every milestone, same answer. I never wavered in my reply. The adults around me chalked it up to precociousness or a flippant fascination with the number. But I knew. I felt it deep in my bones.

2020 is going to be my year.

Cut to New Year's Eve, 2019. As the clock strikes midnight, I feel something click deep in my being. A profound knowing that this year will be important, transformative, destined even. Damn, I think. My six-year-old self was really onto something. 2020 is really going to be my year.

Eighteen hours later, I'm in my happiest place: the audience of a Broadway Theatre. Just as the curtain is about to go up, I start to cough. A dry, incessant cough, unlike anything I've ever experienced before. I'm embarrassed – I try to avoid public places when I'm sick. But so far it's just a cough. I feel fine otherwise. I think it might be allergies.

It isn't allergies. I wake up in the middle of the night with a fever. Body aches. Chills. A piercing headache. I sleep it off for the next few days. As my fever finally breaks, I notice that I can't taste my food very well – or at all? I'm miserable. But it's just the flu. I soon forget I was even sick. 2020 can still be my year.

Two months later, I hear the word coronavirus for the first time. And the world falls apart.

It happens slowly, almost imperceptibly, at first. Then at warp speed. With each passing day, the streets of New York City are peppered with more makeshift masks and latex gloves. I'm in utter disbelief. I scoff when I hear that my neighbor is hoarding canned food and toilet paper. "Got enough for six months!" she says. I think she's nuts. I refuse to give into the fear we're being sold.

And still, I notice the way my body clenches when the woman behind me in line at the coffee shop starts to cough. I try to buy hand sanitizer – just in case – but it's sold out everywhere. I instinctively reach for a basket in the grocery store but stop short. Better safe than sorry. It's getting harder to cling to my denial.

Businesses start closing one by one, knocked down in quick succession like a line of dominos. First sporting events and concerts, then bars and restaurants, then schools, then my beloved Broadway. And finally, the official word from the governor: lockdown. Here it is again: the knowing. But this time, it's accompanied by a pit in my stomach.

This is the milestone my younger self was tuned to. Apparently, it is not the expected euphoria of my every dream coming true, (ugh), but the sacrifice of my individual freedom and achievement for collective well-being. A crucial and inescapable item on my soul's cosmic to-do list. Once written in invisible ink, it now glares at me in big, red letters, an unexpected invoice with a deadline already past due. The ancient, eternal part of me remembers the karmic agreement I made. She remembers the original, 'Yes,' my soul said to being alive at this time. But the human part of me is pissed. 2020 was going to be my year.

I try to make the best of it. I will lose 30 pounds! I will write the next great American novel! I will learn to bake!

I set up Zoom appointments with friends and family I've lost touch with and play with green screen backgrounds as a creative outlet. But the novelty wears off and my time quickly devolves into endless scrolling and television binges. Yes Netflix, I'm still here, stop judging me.

I crawl down some conspiracy rabbit holes. Not enough to permanently alter my sense of reality, but enough to find the sliver of security they offer. In the face of debilitating chaos, even an evil plot feels like order.

I decide that if I have to grieve, then I will do it under the cherry blossoms. I park myself on a bench in Central Park by the Alice in Wonderland statue and cry. Weep really. I almost resent that my face mask hides my tears. I want to be seen in my devastation. I watch as person after person walks past me. Some attempt to comfort me with gestures. A thumb's up, a hand on their heart. But mostly they avoid making eye contact. As if any sort of human acknowledgement might be infectious.

I kneel in silence at a vigil honoring George Floyd. 8 minutes and 46 seconds. The only sounds in the courtyard are the whir of a patrolling police helicopter overhead and the loud chirping of a single robin in the trees above us. A sharp clash between our man-made disorder and our truest, natural essence. God, our culture's priorities are for the birds, I think.

I can't remember the last time I saw a real-life, human, in the flesh smile. The robotic delays on video calls and the pervasive expressionlessness of face masks exhaust me. Watching the people around me pass off pale facsimiles of connection as the real thing infuriates me. I have never felt more lonely.

I swear, 2020 was going to be my year.

It starts to occur to me that my decision to tough it out alone in the epicenter of the pandemic was not a good one. I have a meme-inspired epiphany. (Aren't they all in 2020?) I remember I'm allowed to change my mind; make a new plan. Armed by my angels with positive affirmations and anti-viral aura spray, I fly home on a one-way ticket. The tricky web of family dynamics is finally preferable to isolation.

I spend my fourteen-day government-mandated quarantine in my parents' basement. Food is lowered to me from the main level in a dumbwaiter Dad expertly fashioned with a bucket and some rope. It feels good to be cared for. To not have to go it alone. I read by the pool, cuddle with our dog, watch sunsets over the lake. I laugh and occasionally bicker with my family from six feet away.

2020 is starting to feel like my year again.

But then Dad collapses on our kitchen floor. There are still other health risks beyond the virus, it turns out. The paramedics wheel him out of my childhood home on a gurney and close the ambulance door with him inside it. Conscious, but barely. Completely alone. We aren't allowed to stay with him. Hours pass before I get a nurse on the phone to confirm that he's still alive. He's stable, he'll survive, but his heartbeat is irregular. And he's delirious. "It's the weirdest thing," she says. "He knows the exact date, but not the year. He keeps insisting we're in 1914." I startle myself and the nurse on the other end of the line when I laugh. I admire his mind's chronological self-preservation instincts. 2020 is definitely not our year.

Soon after, our family cat dies. Because morbid irony abounds in 2020. She is lying in my lap on our living room floor as she takes her last breath. Her slip from this world to the next is strangely anticlimactic – so subtle that I wasn't even sure it had really happened. I keep petting her, waiting for some authority figure to swoop in and pronounce her dead. No-one comes. I have to call it myself.

And somewhere in the mix of all this were the wildfires and the hurricanes and the high stakes do-or-die presidential elections. Oh and murder hornets! Remember murder hornets?!

So, no, 2020 was objectively not my year.

I feel naïve to have missed the mark so spectacularly. How could I have been so wrong about what this year would be? I beat myself up; I really should have known. I read the celestial predictions for 2020, littered with words like destruction. Constraint. Power struggle. Was it hubris that allowed me to believe that fate would somehow skip me? Or fear? Two sides of the same coin, I guess.

My journey has been mild in the grand scheme of things. I know this. But still I fight for my particular pain to be honored. I feel invisible in the ceaseless wave of collective experience. Universal oneness – the goal I'm told – feels like a stamping out, a glossing over. It seems that the only way to exist this year is to be part of the amorphous 'we'. A neglected part of me screams to be noticed, embarrassingly bratty in her delivery. Tell me I'm special! Tell me I matter! I want to be singular. I want to be unique. But it doesn't feel like there's any room for me. It feels like I'm slipping away.

And suddenly, there she is, crystal clear in my mind's eye. Just when I need her most. The young, innocent me. So connected, so in tune, so wise beyond her years that she somehow remembered a year she hadn't lived yet. I feel the magic and divine order woven inextricably into her being; the perfect consecration of her existence. She's the distinctive spark of life I came to be. The rush I feel trapped under isn't hers. She is calm. Patient. Certain. How strange to have lost her this year of all years. How beautiful to find her again.

I am reminded that the universe began as a tiny speck. Galaxies upon galaxies folded in on top of each other. The entire expanse of everything that exists waiting as pure potential on the head of a pin. Cramped, restricted, chafing against the edges of its reality. (Sounds a lot like 2020, doesn't it?) Until – bang! Creation. Space. Beginning. The explosion, it turns out, is not the apocalypse, but a fresh start. A new vantage point from which an infinite number of futures can be created. I suspect now that my knowing wasn't pointing to a finish line at all, but a new year zero. It feels like freedom.

From that perspective, it seems downright laughable that I would pin the weight of my unrealized dreams on the flip of a calendar page. I'm adorable in my misguidedness. But I can already feel a wave of amnesia creeping in, obscuring my hard-earned wisdom once again. The pristine blank page urges me to proclaim, "2021 is definitely going to be my year!"

I won't do it. I will let my life unfold outside of time. But if you ever hear me say it again, pinch me or something, would you? I'll thank you later, I promise.

SARAH WEALE

Witty commentary meets grounded spirituality, Sarah Weale is a writer, astrologer and transformational coach.

Through personal revelations and experienced mentorship, she helps you move from confusion to clarity for a more meaningful and fulfilling life. She is as willing to mine the emotional depths as she is to laugh through hard times and is committed to a version of personal development that allows for both.

Come visit her little corner of the internet:
www.sarahweale.com
@sarah.weale on Instagram

2020: THANK YOU
by Sarah Lloyd

....

I hear so many people cursing 2020; saying it was a waste of a year, an awful time; grief and loss at what used to be, and grief for those who have left us to hang with angels.

I can see it was difficult for many, the forced alone time, the lack of opportunities to socialise, travel, fulfil our work dreams, do all the things we had planned.

What I do see is a lack of gratitude for what we HAVE experienced this year – that inability to reframe, and just sit and absorb what we are being spoon fed. And you know what it frustrates the hell out of me...I digress.

I hadn't really figured out what I was going to do this year, well certainly past March. Weirdly, I had been approached with opportunities past that point and most of them didn't sit right. Whether it was intuition kicking in, but in my body, I just knew not to make any firm plans.

If I had carried on as I had done in March, I would be burnt out to a crisp by now at any rate.

2020 was the year I launched my book, in the place where the seed took root. On 1st Feb, she landed, whilst I was hanging with my magical friends in Glastonbury. All the feels. Then I got to hang out and support clients and take my book to the Mindful Living Show in early March. I had no clue that the connections I made there would be integral to this year. But they were. I also got to skip out on a girlie weekend just before we locked down for good – so my cup was full by the time the world stopped.

Those first few weeks, moving from having the whole house to myself whilst the children and husband where at school and work, I can't lie, were difficult for me. Before our worlds collided, I realise now that I had two versions of me.

Magical me – tree hugging, rituals, meditation, and working with magical clients – the stuff I filled up on. I changed my life so I could feel lit up and high vibe when I went to 'work'.

And 3D me – mum, wife, cook, cleaner, playmate and schoolteacher. Like Mary Poppins, only less fun, snappish, crazier hair and sporting the same pair of jeans for weeks on end.

The big lesson for me this year has been about bringing those two versions of me, under one Sarah shaped umbrella. Integrating magical me, with mummy me. It has been challenging at times… especially when you start a meditation, you just get to the point where you are about to astral travel with your guides and then the door flings open, with a demand for a snack.

The hammock, which I ordered in April, was the saviour for this situation. I found myself getting a good hour of quiet time once that was installed – and I know hubs did too.

It is our holiday from life place.

So back to March, before it all kicked off. One of the connections I had made was with a radio station – Wellbeing Radio, who had invited me to have my own show. Honoured, humbled and flattered, something inside told me to take it and see what occurred. No attachment, really just going with flow on this one, I accepted and started recording and airing my show from the middle of April.

This opportunity, I realise now, helped me to expand my view of the world.

Here I was needing to talk about something meaningful each week about what I did for a living. At first the task felt overwhelming but the more shows I recorded, the braver I got. This, ritual, gave me purpose and a voice at a time when I, and others needed it most.

Don't get me wrong I had my moments. Those deep dark moments. When you feel your breath is caught in your ribs. You feel like you are going to combust and all you want to do is walk out that front door and run as far away from the reality that you are living.

It was those moments, when I realised I need to dig deep. So, fucking deep.

I learned so much about myself, my husband and my children. I realised that we, as parents, needed to model our behaviour, so the children would learn from us.

Our first few weeks of home schooling were fun to start with – kind of like a honeymoon period that was new for all of us. Then came the realisation that things where not going to go back to how they were, the kids couldn't see their friends, or their grandparents.

Grief, anger and sorrow raged in different forms.

Both of us; trying to keep calm, juggle our work commitments – luckily it was a little easier for me, as some of my client work had wrapped up, so I had space to take care of the children. BUT trying to schedule in self-care when everyone is home was near on impossible.

Cue hammock time.

At times it felt like we were in a war – a war with an unknown entity. Deep in the trenches, stockpiling food, all the disaster movies where the family is against the world played in my mind.

"Would we all start turning into zombies?"

I totally bought into the fear for the first few weeks, standing outside clapping the NHS and dutifully posting rainbow pictures on our windows. The children writing letters and drawing pictures to be posted to those we were missing.

Our main priority was to keep the family safe, bellies full and stay as calm as we possibly could. Reiki and my energy work played a big part. I would regularly Reiki and sage our house, send the children energy bubbles, and distance healing to the family I couldn't see.

Grounding in nature, allowing the tears and emotions flow. We each allowed ourselves to feel.

We began to focus on what was truly important – schooling was kept to maths and English; we huggled on the sofa watching films; made dens and played games in the sunshine in our garden; planted seeds and enjoyed harvesting our home-grown cucumbers, tomatoes and lettuce. In our bubble at that time, it really brought us closer together.

It was only when Dominic Cummings, the PM's PR Guy, made the press following his trip to his mother's halfway across the country did I start to smell a rat. Being in PR and having worked in corporate environments you know the number one priority is to preserve brand reputation. In order to do this, you get to know ALL the deep dark and dirty secrets because that's how you manage the smoke, should it start to billow.

That is when I started to question what the mainstream media was telling us. Here was the guy who knew all the facts, acting like it was ok to travel, break the guidelines etc… Of course, he has been fired now six months later, but even so. He knew the 'risks' and it dawned on me that the risks were not as bad as we had been led to believe.

It wasn't that I didn't believe there was a virus, one that could kill someone with a low immune system, but it was how it was being dealt with. I found myself researching other schools of thought, knowing in my gut I wouldn't be alone in this theory.

Sure enough, people started to come out of the woodwork, speaking against the government, the medical advisers. I found myself having deep conversations with my husband over the 'conspiracies' and the possible reasons why this was occurring.

It was freeing. But also, deeply unnerving. It was the matrix of everything we have ever been told unravelling right before our very eyes if you allowed yourself to look closely.

It is everything the spiritual community talks about – that everything is an illusion – attachment and control – lead to fear and disappointment.

To live a love-filled life is to see the abundance that we have been blessed with. And here in 2020 we had been given that chance. Whether to embrace and cherish this thing called life, or live in fear of something that we are being told is dangerous, and hide behind out masks.

It felt like the scales had dropped from my eyes. It made me realise that there IS always another way – the road less travelled. The masks I bought went back in the cupboard, I decided I would make myself exempt from the madness.

I felt brave, in my power, and more me than I had ever done.

Before you stone me for throwing off my mask dear reader, I social distance (I don't like touching strangers anyway. In fact, I actually love queues and limits on numbers of people in shops and restaurants....), I wash my hands and my household is dosed up on more vitamin D than you can shake a stick at.

So once that realisation had dropped in for me, it felt like I was soaring above watching from the sky.

I felt this sense of relief, that I didn't have to reignite social relationships, I didn't need to go to a pub ever again, I could let all of that go. I could spend time with people I actually felt equal and aligned with.

It was a relief when the schools returned, by this point I knew the children needed to be around their friends. I think also we are very lucky in that the school had a headteacher committed to ensuring children's mental health is a priority. *Though the screams when both children are asked to wash their hands would suggest that habit will scar them for life.*

Summer came, and we had booked trips down to the coast. It was the change of scene we needed. A new four walls to call home, blessed with beautiful weather, as we had been since April – another saving grace through all the rules and regulations. We visited some of the places I had been to as a child and I felt a deep connection and healing during those visits.

We had lots of fun too, the four of us, a unit, a team.

Working with each of our needs to rest and play.

We as a family grew together. Sometimes it was ugly, sometimes it was painful, most of the time it was real. Transformational time with my husband and my two girls, and for that time we spent, I will be forever grateful.

And as I start to close off my 2020 vision, it is one of deep gratitude for the connections that were made especially this year. As a business owner, there was a fleeting feeling that I should have done more, pivoted quicker. Competitiveness and a dash of loneliness crept in there too. But what I see as I reflect on the whole year, once I removed myself from the 'pandemic problem'; I actually opened myself up to the whole universe.

Sparking connections with like-minded business owners, people really in alignment with their hearts and souls' mission.

It has shone a light on my purpose, which is to uncover and speak the truth in the media, to forge a new way, a new earth – one where we all live, love and co-exist in harmony without fear, control or agenda.

I see new publications; radio stations and businesses springing up, all thinking in a new way. I see the harmony struck when two businesses support each other, and the greatness they can achieve.

2020 has truly been that time in the mud, uncomfortable, deeply painful at times; but it has been a transformational one.

One that is certainly allowing me to live and think in an unbound way. With no limits, no fear, no judgement; only love for oneself and one another. All equal. All powerful.

2021 is just the beginning. And so it is.

SARAH LLOYD

In the media and PR business for 23 years, Sarah Lloyd quit her global corporate role in 2017, in a bid to be a master of her own and to bring a better balance to her life, which led her to setting up her own PR and Brand Consultancy – IndigoSoulPR. An intuitive and Reiki Energy Master herself, she specialises in working in 'flow' so has thrown the rule book out the window. Her mission is to teach and guide others to share their stories, without fear, on their terms.

Specialising in her own brand of magic-based, conscious PR and communications – her Alchemy strategy sessions help to ignite the fire within, acknowledge blocks, and help to transmute all that has held clients back from stepping up and sharing their mission and purpose.

She is a graduate of the SEED Network – led by author and Women's Empowerment Guru Lynne Franks. In March 2020, her book Connecting the Dots – 'A Guide to making Magic with the Media' was published via the Unbound Press.

She is a radio presenter on Wellbeing Radio – her show 'Connecting the Dots' explores all the ways to share your story on your terms in all areas of your life. Features editor of online spiritual title UnTamed Soul; and Publicist for The Unbound Press and That Guys House Publishing House. And in 2020 became the judge of best spiritual brand for the Soul & Spirit Awards.

She has worked with a mix of clients – including authors and entrepreneurs, as well as small and large businesses – to build awareness of their brands and products in a magical and purposeful way. When not working, Sarah can be found at the bottom of the garden pottering about in the greenhouse, dropping crystals at sacred sites, attempting to practice Yoga, or outside enjoying the countryside with her two girls.

Find out more at:
https://indigosoulpr.com

IF YOU DON'T EXPERIENCE LIFE, YOU CAN'T WRITE ABOUT IT
by Lorraine Pannetier

....

2020 was the year that brought me back to life.

The year that gifted me the most profound, transformational gift possible to any human being. The gift of pure, unconditional love.

And yet, this isn't a simple romantic story of falling in love, with a Hollywood cliché ending.

It's a story that goes beyond the depths of space and time to reunite a Starseed soul with her true purpose.

....

Meeting my twin flame didn't happen overnight. A chemical reaction took place at some point in the history of the galaxies. Planets collided, stars exploded and atoms split.

A spark. A slow burn. A flame.

At the end of 2019, I broke my ankle whilst settling my daughter into her first year university accommodation. With an insignificant slip on a damp pavement, a loud crack and an instant feeling of nausea, something in the Universe shifted as subtly as the bones in my left ankle.

In the weeks that followed, stuck indoors with an inflatable boot, crutches and a never-ending creativity in how to make food while balanced on one leg and then transport it to the lounge, I decided I was ready to give up the struggle.

I'd had enough.

I'd spent over eight years as a single parent, only ever making 'just enough' money to make ends meet. A rising cost of living meant that the luxuries had slowly been eliminated. No more chiropractic treatments, massage or nice moisturiser. While much of it had been an essential and exciting budgeting learning curve, it left me with a deep-rooted fear of truly looking after and loving myself.

I no longer enjoyed the playful nature of clothes shopping or the curiosity in discovering this season's make-up colour trends. I stopped dancing around the house. I lost the joy in washing my hair. And I rarely went out – partly through a lack of money but also because I'd forgotten how to enjoy social situations.

I was lost.

Or rather, I had lost myself.

And so, breaking my ankle forced me to sit still, accept help and truly embrace my vulnerability. I decided in that moment that it was time to put me first again. To nurture the beautiful soul within me and the human body that craved sensual touch and abandoned excitement.

I wanted to hang out with the wild woman within me. This gorgeous goddess that held the key to my ability to truly savour everything this lifetime had to offer.

I was ready to let love into my life in every corner of my world and every facet of my being. Within mere moments of setting the intention, the Universe showed up with the support I needed: a sisterhood of women in a monthly membership group, connections to new, beautiful souls and then, just a few weeks later, my twin flame showed up.

Except, I didn't know that at the time. Neither of us did.

He made his way firmly into my heart within days of our deep, intimate online chats. He was ready to get to know the *real* me. He wasn't interested in the superficial and he definitely wasn't playing games. He simply wanted to peel back the layers and reveal my fears, my insecurities, my joys and my passions.

With every soft, delicate layer he removed, our connection strengthened.

For the first time in my life, I'd met a man who showed up consistently, every single day. Always a good morning and a good night. Humour, interesting conversations, stories about his day and random GIFs. Digital dating at its best.

Flights were booked to meet in person in early March and our first meeting was laced with a powerful, yet gentle curiosity. We touched hands. We laughed and smiled. We walked in the wind, and took selfies by the sea. We drank tea on the sofa and talked about life.

Twelve hours after meeting, we had our first kiss. My feminine intuition allowing him to lead our connection wherever it wanted to go.

Within days of our first weekend together, the world shut down.

Coronavirus swooped in and threw us all into a new paradigm; a new way of being.

Parents battled home-schooling their children. Office workers struggled with technology. Restaurants and bars closed their doors.

Suddenly everyone knew about Zoom.

For me, little changed. I continued to work from home and my youngest teenage daughter settled back into home learning. My eldest returned from university and we got into a new routine of food shopping deliveries, doing our own cleaning (or not!) and the occasional Indian takeaway to break the monotony.

My man was my rock and my saviour throughout. He was always there with deep understanding, kindness and humour.

There was no need for me to ever doubt his feelings – and yet of course, I did. Twin flames are sent as a mirror to help us grow, learn and transform.

The misunderstandings felt like drowning in a black swamp of goo.

In truth, we were both triggered by random words that struck us like an arrow to the heart. For me, this brought up old wounds, old patterns, old behaviours.

I never liked the version of me that reacted in this way. The 'me' who got scared about him meeting someone younger, slimmer, more wild, more of a water baby, more of a dog lover, more into snowboarding. Someone without kids, a house and bills to pay. Someone who could fly to Bali for epic adventures at a moment's notice.

All negative, fear-based thoughts that triggered me to over react or back off.

And yet, every time I backed off or went quiet in a Facebook Messenger conversation, he'd be there with a hug. It was like he instinctively knew what I needed. I never wanted to push him away. I wanted him to hold me close. And never let go.

As lockdown restrictions eased in July, we enjoyed a long weekend in a lush Airbnb property in a beautiful forest. It was everything we both needed. Cosy fireplace chats and wild sexual chemistry. The kind of intimate connection that opens you up to new levels and brings a sense of coming home amidst the ultimate freedom.

Over the summer months, we enjoyed more weeks together with beach trips and new experiences. Watching the moonrise over the horizon, on a clear, star-filled night, sat on the beach wrapped in blankets was definitely one of our highlights.

At my home together, we worked on client projects while sharing intimate kisses and cups of tea at random moments. We showed each other it was possible to run a business *and* enjoy a healthy, satisfying relationship. It never had to be one or the other.

We gave each other hope.

We showed each other love in ways we'd never experienced before.

We filled each other's lives with small moments of joy; little pockets of happiness in a crazy world. And it was beautiful.

But just as dark clouds pass in front of the sun, so twin flame relationships ignite something in us that we can no longer ignore.

For many years I'd experienced a deep sense of longing and could never quite get to the bottom of why I felt that way.

The Universe knew I needed something that would shake me to my core – and it had to be unexpected and delivered from a place of pure, unconditional love.

It had to be something that would transform me forever.

It might leave me temporarily bruised, battered and broken, but ultimately stronger, more beautiful and more filled with love than ever before.

He had to leave.

It wasn't a break-up in the usual sense, just a deep-rooted knowing and intuition on both sides that we'd come to an impasse. We had no idea whether to go up, over or around – we just knew we were stuck.

It happened so quickly, so suddenly.

As the tears flowed and we held each other tight, we said, 'I love you,' face to face for the first time.

And we both knew it was the absolute truth.

Our hands held each other's faces and we sobbed messy tears.

I love you.

I love you.

It was an ending neither of us expected, and yet in our heart-breaking, gut-wrenching pain, we knew somehow that it was the right thing to do.

He flew back to the UK that morning and while he navigated planes, trains and somewhere to stay, I flitted between moments of deep clarity and dark moments of untamed sadness.

The next morning in the shower, and for the first time in years, it all come out. As the water ran over my naked, curvy body that had been held so tightly, romantically and sexually the night before, the tears began to pour out.

All the fears, struggles and challenges I'd faced, I let it all go.

I sobbed.

It wasn't pretty.

And yet I knew it was what I needed.

As the gratitude for this moment I'd been given rolled in, I realised this was my, 'Eat, Pray, Love,' moment.

I surrendered to the universe with an inner knowing that I'd be OK.

Except, I knew I didn't want to be, 'just OK.' I wanted to thrive. I wanted to fly.

In the days that followed, we talked about what we were going through. We shared our feelings, our love and our gratitude for each other.

The love hadn't gone anywhere – we just changed the shape of the container it was in.

And then he wrote me a story…

A story where a struggling human had been able to find his heart through the love I'd shown him. That he had been opened up to love after being closed for so long. That he could now feel and had been given hope, light and a reason to live.

He'd been given the gift of true love, entirely unexpectedly.

It would be easy to think that this was the gift I'd been given. To know that I'd helped someone to experience that kind of love.

Except with a twin flame, it's never that simple.

And the love goes both ways.

He continued his story with a twist…

Unlike in the movies where the little Starseed would morph into that bright star she is and fly off into the sky as the film ends, giving the viewer a warm glow and a contented feeling of a journey completed, that wasn't about to happen.

Instead, what the Starseed had missed was that this was actually her journey all along – not about the human she'd given her gift to.

Her human had come all this way to be with her at this exact moment in time where he could give her his gift and watch her fly.

She felt for the first time like she actually belonged and knew her purpose. She opened her heart to the full experience of being human.

She cried and laughed simultaneously and felt this heavy weight lifting from her shoulders.

She knew then that she wasn't here to do just one thing. She was given the gift of a human life to experience even more such moments by being her brilliant, beautiful, bright self.

The little Starseed realised she was enough. Always had been and always will be. All she ever needed to do was to fully embody the little Starseed inside this human form, shining bright.

She realised she could stop trying so hard, give up the struggle and just be herself. This was the Universe's plan all along. A story of her transformation. A transformation that would set her free, to transmute her gift in exciting ways to reach out and touch people. Seeing this, she was set free to create and turn her gift into limitless possibilities.

She finally saw the light in herself radiating outwards, filling her soul with everything she'd ever need and an abundance to share with as many people as possible during her time on Earth.

....

As I sit with this story today, I know in my heart that

2020 was so much more than a new chapter. It was a complete plot twist that would transform life forever.

I've been given a gift that will have a ripple effect around the world as I play my small part in shifting human consciousness.

Where my story goes next, and what happens in 2021, no-one knows.

And yet, somehow, I'm filled with more love, peace and lightness than I've ever known before.

I've got this.

You've got this.

And so it is.

LORRAINE PANNETIER

Affectionately known as The Word Whisperer, Lorraine possesses a unique and natural intuitive gift for illuminating her clients' hidden truths and passions, weaving them into words to create engaging content that ensures they radiate confidence and create the impact they desire. Lorraine has a wonderfully nurturing personality, rich in intuitive feminine energy, Starseed wisdom and professional copywriting skills that come together to raise the vibration of the planet and inspire those she reaches.

Find out more at: **https://thesoulfulword.com/**

A HOPE FOR HUMANITY
by Holly McLoughlin

....

There's a deep unrest within my soul. Some days I'm distracted enough by activity to not see it. There are days when it drains me, as I struggle to feel whole. Something was taken from me, something I can't explain. It's an overwhelming grief. Am I a bad person? I must be for these bad things to be happening to me. No-one values me, no-one cares. Everyone leaves me. It's so lonely. I want someone to save me. No-one's ever there for me. Don't be vulnerable, you'll be rejected. I can't be me. The past lives on in my present.

Shut it down. Breathe. It's rising. Anger, actually rage, oh wait some blame. And in ignorance I run. I hide. I must avoid anything that makes it true. Anything that confirms my worst fear, that I am bad, not enough, worthless. Feelings of despair well in my stomach. Muscles clench. No, please, I can't go there. I don't want to be helpless. I want to be strong. Stuff it down into my cells. I know it'll pop up in my eyes as tears when I'm next criticised. It was all too much for me. I didn't understand.

Relief. That voice is here. You're disgusting with that secret. You can never be honest because of it. No-one will ever know you fully because of it. If your parents didn't love you how will anyone else? You just be sensible now. Don't be who you are, you're lazy. You could never do that, you're too impatient. Why would you want to do that? It's evil and immoral. Money doesn't grow on trees you know. Who do you think you are? You're no expert. You're selfish. You're a dreamer, too idealistic. Agony and yet safety.

I try to go against the voice. When I listen to it I feel constricted and yet safe. When I try to expand my being the anxiety rises. Stuck in the struggle to prove my light. Attempting to conceal all that makes me look bad. Trying, oh so hard, to convince others that I'm not bad. Asking, do you think I'm a bad person? Seeking permission and validation to be me. Angry as I know my intentions were never bad. Confused about why I feel this way. Logically I know I'm fine. Emotionally it's turmoil. When will I be at peace?

One day she came. The nurturing one. She whispered lovingly in my ear. I love you. You are enough. It wasn't your fault. Anger is a natural response to boundaries being crossed. The guilty feeling is someone else's beliefs that you've taken on as your own. I'm here for you now. You can invite the uncomfortable in. Let it be. All parts of you are valid. Your emotions are like little messengers of wisdom, there are no good or bad ones, just little gifts if you can be with them. They will show you the way if you let them.

Knock knock. It's Shame. Oh god not you. I'm here to help. Really? Yes. Let me in. I have a message for you. I'm not sure I want the message but decide it can't be more agony than how things already are. Hi, why are you here I ask? Shame replies to keep you safe. Safe from what? The tellings off, the chaos, the unfairness. Tingling in my nose, my tear ducts flush droplets to my eyes. Oh no. I'm sad. I didn't feel loved. There was no-one to protect me. There was no-one to save me. I didn't know what to do. I felt empty. A walking blank.

Little one, you were abandoned. You made up a lie that it was your fault. It wasn't your fault. It was the wounds of others. I resist the nurturing voice. It's uncomfortable, not what I'm used to. It's unknown to me. 'I love you,' she says. My inner little girl's heart lights up, she feels seen and heard and honoured. Given permission to feel what she feels without judgment. I'm sorry for what happened to you and that I wasn't there for you. You have such a compassionate heart. I realise that I must give to myself what I never received. I am that nurturing voice. The longing to be loved is quenched by me, my self-nurturer.

All the running, what was it from? From my inner child and her pain. I'd cast her away so as to survive. Now she's coming back to me. Integrating with me. Showing me her sweet wisdom through the emotions. I'm listening. I can be with her. She expresses her rage, her pains, her loneliness. We are loved. We are nurturing self-worth. We belong. We are integrating as one. Life is happening with uncomfortable ease. It's strange. I'm more familiar with drama and struggle. I release it.

In the light of pure love, life becomes a work of art. Living life from the heart. I see now how the pain has been a gift. You see I was initiated far too young. It came as a shock. I was unprepared and didn't expect it. I didn't understand what it was about. I didn't have the words even to describe it. It was done at the wrong time, by the wrong person, in the wrong way, with the wrong intent, on the wrong person. It was sexual abuse. Stage one began. I was separated. Isolated. Alone. Cut off. The trust was betrayed. The world made no sense. The initiation had begun.

The prolonged ordeal left its invisible scars long after the acts. My solitary journey was now in phase two. I was in pain, I was terrified. There was no safe container of elders to support me, no watchful eyes to keep me safe. There was no end in sight. I thought I would remain in separation forever. Always being ashamed of myself. The unwelcome touch had left my spirit separated from my body. No safety hatch. No guidance. Pure confusion about how to be at peace with myself. It was a traumatic brush with death. My body was alive, but it was without spirit. Like walking round empty, hollow, dazed.

Stage three was supposed to come. No-one told me I had survived the ordeal and came out the other side a new being. No-one mourned my sudden loss of childhood. No-one recognised I was a changed person. No-one welcomed me home as a valued member of the clan. No-one celebrated with me. Instead the ordeal was kept secret. It lay in the shadows for nearly thirty years. When it was brought to light, the clan rejected me. It was too painful, too unbearable. I was cast adrift in the shadows of what couldn't be faced.

I was stuck between worlds. The horror had happened, there was no protective ceremony, no overseer of the process and no welcoming back. There was no way for me to take my conscious place as a member of society. I was in limbo, unfinished, cycling between stage one and two with no way out. I longed with every molecule of my being to be accepted. To feel normal. To not be an outcast and separate. 2020 has been about finding my tribe. The places where I'm welcomed. And making up my own ritual to complete stage three.

So here is my ritual, with my inner nurturer, trust and intuition as guides...

I realise that I survived my death-like ordeal. My inner child died through separation when I was sexually abused. This year I have grieved for myself. I cried sobbing childlike tears. I gave myself permission to feel my anger. There were no words, I just made random sounds to feel it, express it and release it. I offered myself compassion rather than blame. I made sense of my victim story and in that process saw my core lie was believing it happened because I was bad.

I had chosen to keep the secret in order to ensure I was loved and not rejected. Perhaps on some level I knew I needed to be welcomed back into society as a fully-fledged new person. Sadly my own family couldn't offer me that when I shared what had happened. With it being such a taboo subject still, there was certainly no celebration of my triumph. However, I am claiming my grace, my divine joy for a life of connection, growth and acceptance. I embrace all of the gifts that my initiation has given me and will put them to use.

I share this story firstly for myself. To have it accepted in the *#2020VISION* book can be my moment of being welcomed back home by the tribe. It is a physical marker of my inward movement to become the changed me. No longer a survivor but a thriver. I choose to be me, healed and whole. I ask you to celebrate with me. To be joyful in bringing this story out of the shadow and into the light. To help me to heal fully. To be in completeness and peace once more. It would be a gift like no other.

I share this story secondly for other women who have experienced childhood sexual trauma. I hope these brief words offer you guidance and hope, that you too will be guided to healing and wholeness. The separation experienced, no matter the extremity of the abuse, is equally painful to us all. I want you to know that it was not your fault. That you have survived and come through the experience being forever changed. We welcome you and value you as part of society and as a new person. We celebrate all that you are, the fullness of your being, with those scars that may not be visible.

I started my unbound writing journey a year ago. My first vision was to write something for women who have been through this abuse. Today that vision is fulfilled. They say writing to heal others heals you in the process, and that has certainly been my personal experience.

Write and write and write it all out. Make sense of all that happened to you, find your grace in it, and return to us. We are incomplete without you. It is my deepest hope that these wounds are healed for all humanity.

Finally, I offer deepest forgiveness to all who have harmed me, my ancestors, or any being through sexual abuse and abandonment. That is not to say what they did was right, rather that I am no longer willing to carry the pain and burden of this wound with me. The ordeal is over. I am renewed. I am excited for all that life has to offer and am now free to live a whole and blessed life. You are too.

This is how 2020 transformed me.

Thank you, thank you, thank you.

Greatest love, greatest love, greatest love.

HOLLY MCLOUGHLIN

Holly McLoughlin guides evolving leaders to show up fully expressed as their real selves in work, with their full emotional range and self-belief. Her vision is for a world where leaders at all levels can truly nurture others and the planet. Holly believes this starts with your personal culture and finding the gifts in your unique story.

If you struggle to connect with a vision for your life's work, or long to align your thinking, feeling and behaviours with your intentions, there is healing to be done so that you can make an impact in the world. You can find out more about Holly's work at the website **www.evolving.careers** and discover how to drop the striving, so that you can start thriving, as the truly empowered person you are born to be.

HOMECOMING
by Moriah Ama Hope

....

Wow, 2020, you have been the best and the worst of times all rolled into one. A real doozy!

There has been no other year like it. It has to be official, I'm sure it's official, right?

The chaos, confusion, misinformation, gut wrenching grief, stark extremes and polarities everywhere we look. The loss of identities, sureties, lives, loved ones, liberties, occupations, our pictures of reality, our dreams and plans, incomes and daily routines. Separation at its most extreme, stripping us bare of what we hold most dear. All turned upside down and inside out. Wrung out to dry. Dishevelled and bewildered.

And at the same time, through the dark, murky waters and the chaos,

++ there is a hint, a spark of hope and renewal, the tiniest glimmer of a new dawn and a glimpse of what could be. A new way of relating, a renewed commitment to those we hold most dear, a revision of our values and dreams. A new Earth in the birthing.

Like the proverbial caterpillar we have been squeezed, coerced, broken down, our very constitution re-assembled so that we can emerge into a new form, a new life and a new way of relating with ourselves, life, the planet and each other.

It's clear that the world as we knew it was broken and not working for the whole and the planet, but for the few and for materialism. A shift needed to happen. Few could have predicted quite how this might happen.

And so here we are, at the end of 2020. All making our way through our metamorphosis. Individually and collectively. A process of collective re-emergence like no other in living memory.

For me, it has been an opportunity to get truly focused on giving structure to the creative projects that I have felt hovering around me for a while now, tapping on my head and my shoulder like little birds wanting attention and food. "Me next. Feed me," they chirp into my ear.

I have had to be clear, focused, discerning and above all structured. Structure and discipline do not come easily to me. I prefer free-wheeling, exploring and deep diving so it has been a revelation that I have discovered new ways of being and working. And, despite the sheer discomfort of "pinning myself down to my chair and laptop," I have discovered that structure, discipline and commitment could be my greatest allies. A revelation. Who knew?

I have also had to face my shadows many times over. For me this has manifested as sadness, grief, frustration and anger. I cannot come and go as I wish. I value freedom and variety and have felt bereft at the sheer routine, predictability of my days in lockdown – variety is high on my values list too. I have felt disempowered, controlled, despondent. I have felt at times like a prisoner in my own home. I didn't see my ageing parents for nine months and my adult sons for months at a time. I barely saw friends all year. No hugs, no physical contact. Unthinkable before this pandemic. Our sense of touch denied. Connection thwarted. Loved ones seriously ill. Overwhelm was a frequent visitor.

I have danced with my shadows for years and this year I have felt their presence even more acutely. Suppressed childhood feelings of isolation, sadness, separation, lack of belonging, feeling lost, left out and misunderstood. The weird one in the family.

So, I am learning to be present for these feelings. Cry when I need to, express them when I need to, listen attentively and follow through with action, be in nature and naps – lots of naps!

I gave myself permission to be in a "funk." A gloriously messy, grumpy, tearful, sloth-like funk. Allowing myself to wallow in it for longer than my mind suggested it was OK to. Mind suggested it was lazy, self-indulgent to stay in this state. Surely, I should shift myself out of it and "pull myself together"? Mind said that I should know better. It warned that if I stay in this funk for too long that I would never find my way out of it. I would drown, be swallowed up and lose myself, lose my way.

I consciously chose to stay in the funk. To wallow until I emerged the other side of it. However long it took. I would not judge it or me, not chase it away, wish it gone or make an enemy of it.

And herein lies the jewel in the cave of longing.

This has been one of my most visceral learnings of 2020. When I have allowed all my feelings to be present, without judgement or conditions, something truly magical happens. They rise to the surface and then they melt.

Like icebergs and shards, deeply buried and hurting like hell, when we cease making an enemy of them, they cease to have power over us. There is no "them and us." It is all US.

In the year of feeling "stuck at home," the true gift was that I came home to myself.

Priceless. Unexpected.

As we complete this year and nudge into 2021, there are now many more known unknowns than there are knowns. Our life as we knew it has changed. Irrevocably in many cases.

Let's welcome our edges, our soft underbelly vulnerabilities and let's welcome our fears and our feelings as dear friends.

Let's endeavour to make peace with everything we feel, all of our thoughts, our insecurities, our sense of loss.

Let's beckon them closer and hold them as we would a child.

Let's be kind to ourselves and to others.

Let's be in this world but not of it. Feeling it all, staying grounded in love and taking inspired action to create new solutions and possibilities.

Let's trust in our personal visions, dreams, hopes for the future and take the baby steps needed to realise them, holding them ever so gently, knowing that anything can and possibly will change.

Let's make a shift from Me to WE.

Let's pivot into service and ask ourselves, "How can I serve today?"

Let's build new, compassionate, collaborative, inclusive and creative communities around us to help ourselves and each other thrive.

Let's listen deeply, witness without judging, soften our edges, open our hearts and nuzzle into the creativity and innovation that wants to be birthed through us right now.

Let's do this for ourselves.

Let's do it for each other.

Let's come HOME, for in the homecoming there is a peace like no other.

Let's make peace with ourselves and each other.

Let's make peace with life.

Let's come HOME.

MORIAH AMA HOPE

Moriah lives on the south coast of England in West Wittering, close to the beach, where she walks each day.

In 1999, after 15 years in multi-national organisations, she answered a calling to set up her own business, move to the country and spend more time with her young sons.

Moriah has an eclectic tool bag and client base and is passionate about helping her clients to re-invent themselves, their life and their business. She works with energetic blueprints and Deva energies to help birth creative projects into being and is devoted to contributing to co-creating new, evolved, compassionate and collaborative ways of living and working.

In 2017, Moriah published her first oracle deck, "The Magician's Toolkit." She is currently writing her first book due to be published with The Unbound Press in 2021.

Find out more at: **www.amahope.net**

ALCHEMIZE | REVOLUTIONIZE
by Diana Morgan

....

The secret passage to living a fully expressed life is to dream while awake, witnessing with awe as the world conforms to every thought made real.

The connection we have with our own divinity is the most powerful energy in our possession. The ability to harness this energy, and use it in our everyday lives, is what makes us magical creators of our own reality. I believe that each of us have our own unique magic to tap into... learning for ourselves what real flow truly feels like, with pure life force consciously pumping through our veins, in all that we do; a dance that becomes a way of life! Where there are no pieces, no fragments. It is all a flowing whole, and it is taking us on the wild ride of discovering our truest selves.

As we unravel the depths of our inner selves and discover our unique medicine, we can then more powerfully contribute to collective consciousness.

Rising above differences, it is time to do our part in being the positive change that we are here to create.

Near the end of 2011, when I was living in Chicago, before fully understanding or developing my sixth sense, I had a vision while awake. I could see and feel the current societal structures falling away, and it was like the earth was trembling, aching to break through all of the concrete that humans had poured upon her... I felt mass chaos, the pulling apart of families and corporations, a lack of resources, and overall complete turmoil. I saw a division, the dividing line, between one reality and another, and the image was so clear that it has been a driving force in the back of my mind since then. To the left of my vision was FEAR, dark and gloomy, full of pain and lack and suffering. To the right of my vision was LOVE, bright and shining, full of warmth and healing and possibility. In the middle was a definitive line. Yet the line was not thick. It was clear that in between this dark reality and bright reality was one simple choice. Allowing consciousness to be overpowered by fear, or opening up the heart to love and letting it shine in from all directions. One choice felt tightening and claustrophobic, and the other felt expansive, freer, more alive. I was shown this image in a way that struck me like a slap in the face, and I knew that I had some changes to make in my life. This imminent truth, that I was seeing so clearly and feeling so deeply in my bones, did not make much sense to me at the time. But I have revisited it over the years since then, and have found myself sharing it with friends and family many times. Choosing love has been a core focal point that my mind frequently visits.

My visions go beyond that of the present moment, while also being completely immersed in the present moment. There must be destruction for there to be new creation. In knowing this and finding peace in it, I tend to observe things from the perspective of self and also the whole, not attaching myself to any emotion.

In March, my partner and I both lost our jobs within the same week. The industries we worked in just stopped, seemingly overnight. We lived in a mould-ridden, rundown apartment across from a highway, where we had to scream just to hear each other while on the front porch. We had just barely been squeaking by with both of our incomes, and times were already stressful. The uncertainty caused some freak out moments, but for the most part we kept it together and trusted that everything would work out. It was the only way to get through.

This year's journey has brought me to deeply knowing and understanding my place in this intricately woven web of life. I see myself as a warrior for love and a bringer of light, a way-shower for a new state of being. It is not for me to further create divisiveness; it is not for me to judge or shame or choose sides, for any reason, in any situation, at any time. If we support division of any kind, then we are actively diminishing our power. What is for me is to place all of my energy into the power of being ALL of who I am. In taking myself by the hand in a new way this year, I have been gifted with the deep knowings my human self has been seeking for most of my adult life. I am here to embody all that I am and most especially all that has been suppressed. I am intention set on fire!

I first made a list of all that I felt was most important to me to have in my life, and most of these things I did not currently have at the time of writing it, but the list covered all aspects. Allowing those words to flow out of me and to become solidified in visual form was the beginning of my inner transformational journey to embodying the energy of the life on that list. I began to prioritize my time and my energy in a new way, where I felt excited by each day and what would unfold as a result of my intentional, focused energy.

As I allowed for my heart and higher self to lead the way, I was able to "sit back" and observe my life with new eyes. I was faced with only the faces of myself, seeing the layers that needed to be peeled off, so that I could become this new version of myself, to step into her world.

There are many ways to peel off the layers we no longer need, and many ways to bring in that which we truly want to experience. For me, it is a continual combination of deep inner work (via energy healing, meditation, nature medicines, intuitive writing, and expressing myself through song, art, and dance) and fully believing in my desire (like declaring to myself and the world that I've "done it" or "am it" before it's technically true!). I choose to challenge myself in my everyday life, and will elect to do things that scare me, until I master them – like riding on the back of a motorcycle at high speeds and feeling as calm as I would if I were sitting in my living room.

I followed the whisper of my soul to connect more deeply with nature, and more often. My partner and I spent multiple days per week hiking off trail in the forest and foraging. I have taken thousands of nature photos, harvested many pounds of wild edible mushrooms, and have added ingredients and knowledge to my healing apothecary. In the woods, my heart comes alive and my body feels strong!

I found myself clearly visualizing the new life I'm creating and my path to leading others up and out on their way to conscious liberation by following their creative dreams. I imagined what it would feel like to BE this version of myself – what it looked like, smelled like, tasted like, how others treated me, how I appeared, spoke, acted, moved.

Spirit says: "Where we focus our energy is so important; it is our life force! Where are you giving away your life force? Is it worth it? Is it an energy exchange? Or are you depleted? Where are the holes in your energy blanket? Can you feel/see them?"

Some things in my life had to go!!! Like people pleasing at the expense of myself. Every time I would do that, it was a bad experience and I would suffer. I had to learn, with the help of my partner, to not do that to myself anymore. I learned how to honor my true wants and needs, which is much better feeling for everyone. And it is way more attractive! Not just to others, either; I became more attracted to myself.

I also experienced surges of rage energy at times, like random flash floods, that felt like ALL the abuse we have endured as a collective whole... ALL the sexual traumas we have suffered, as a result of the suppression of feminine energy... ALL of the ways we have been shamed, blamed, assaulted, tortured, ridiculed, killed... just for being who we are. This rage feels primal and backed by centuries of our ancestors' trapped pain bodies, not ever having an outlet for transmutation and release. Until now.

This imbalance has caused the majority of the problems we have in society. This has affected every person. Where we are now is a pivotal time in the history of humankind, more so than ever before, because we are entering into new territory – of consciousness.

The old ways are dying. The ways our mothers catered to our fathers 24/7 and didn't heed the whispers in their own hearts... The ways our grandmothers fought just to survive, let alone even think about what they would do otherwise... We have been given an immense gift, and we have all the power needed to activate it. The power of our collective LOVE. The power of our individual healing. The vibrational shift that we are creating by simply BEING who we are and emanating our energy out from that place of love and oneness.

Real transformation happens from within first.

Breaking open my own heart and examining the shards has been the most tedious and most rewarding work of my life.

I leaned into fully loving myself and being devoted to honoring all of myself, in all of my rawness.

I began rebuilding the structures within myself. Piece by piece, bit by bit, scouring my internal energy and catching all the snags. When I would run into one, my body would react with emotion, such as crying, to move that energy through. Then the snag would be smoothed over, and that trapped emotion was gone for good.

For so many years, I felt like I was living on a parallel track to my real life, longing to "jump over." It was frustrating and maddening, that this other life was possible, and that for whatever reason, I could not get there. 2020 was the year that I finally jumped from one track to the other!

It is so freeing... letting go of it all... *That* is all we have to do...

As we awaken to our light, all darkness begins to disappear.

Think of yourself as pliable – you can "rearrange yourself a little" and "adjust as necessary." This goes for your physical body and your energy body. Every aspect of ourselves can be tweaked or changed with conscious effort.

What happens when you believe that all things are possible?

The truth of what you know is clouded in judgment. The truth of who you are is never changing.

What I have learned is that my gifts are brought forth by flow, by being my own unique energetic imprint, by sharing my heart, by giving what I can, by trusting that all is well and I am divinely cared for, in every moment.

What gets me going is chasing the feeling of being so alive, so on fire in my heart, being as turned on as I possibly can in each moment, and doing a check-in with my heart center. "How much juicier can this moment get?!"

Once you have the feeling of being so incredibly turned on by every aspect of your life, every minute bringing with it the possibility of an exciting new adventure, you can begin to become the sorceress of your own life. The one you were born to become.

The fruition of my dream visions from the past 5-10 years are all coming together now, in a beautiful sweeping wave. I am connecting on deeper levels with others because I've further deepened my connection with myself. In developing a new inner dialogue with my body, it has also been transforming; I have conversations with my body and ask what it requires. As we up-level, we need better fuel(s). I enjoy watching how my body responds to acknowledging it in a loving way, and what it feels like to elongate and release. My partner and I have grown more into our love, and we have moved into a house in the country that feels like home. This year has also brought along the elements needed to create my dream job. I now spend my work time doing all of the creative things that I love to do!

I had written in a notebook at one point, "When being at home within yourself feels so good that you don't want any outside stimulus, there's no room for anything outside of loving yourself, because loving all of yourself is to love all of others. As they are, in their perfection. As they exist and are meant to exist. And receiving the same in return." And that has been the space I've purposely chosen to swim in!

In any moment that we are present and actively choosing love, we are living our gift. Nature is not fragile. She is a force. Just like you.

Let's join together in dancing on the mountaintops of our own pleasure!

Singing in the streets we have forged with our own desires!

What the spirit of the feminine is asking now...

Give a voice to the parts that reach up and out and tend to pull back. The parts that have **never** gotten to be heard. The parts that are tired, and the parts that feel small. Use this voice to fuel you.

From the purest depths of my heart, I call out to those who also feel the fire, the unyielding feminine energy rising to heal the people and the planet! This is a summoning:

Let her run wild...

Let them whisper as she soars past...

Let her scream...

Let her discover the ancient sound of her own voice!

Let her be naked...

Let her revel in the power of her own aliveness!

Let her take up space...

Let her echo off the walls and proudly show herself off!

Let her soften and flow...

Let her know peace and the strength of her own being!

Let her be.

Let her be you.

She is the way through the journey, and she is inviting you to play.

DIANA MORGAN

Diana Morgan is a weaver of words and worlds, living in the expansive space of possibilities. She has been reading and writing since the age of three – the same year that she had her first out-of-body experience – and has been a poet for as long as she can remember.

Diana has spent the past decade on a profound spiritual healing journey. In addition to practicing as an intuitive energy healer and entheogenic plant ceremony facilitator, she also has 20 years of experience supporting creative entrepreneurs as a business manager, content creator, and brand strategist. Diana has the unique ability to clearly see and unveil the true spirit of people and help them become who they were born to be. She teaches those whose souls whisper for something more and leads them into the fire within their own hearts!

Learn more about Diana and connect with her at **www.ohyesthis.com**.

SPITTING OUT THE GAG OF PATRIARCHY: SPEAKING TRUTH AND COURAGE IN 2020
by Sarah Wheeler

....

It has been a fucking year.

Gently place your palm down on your heart, close your eyes if you like, take a slow full breath in through your nose feeling your body expand, exhale slowly and completely feeling your body soften. Tune into that place under your hands, the cavern of the very back of your heart. Does any guidance or message come through for you? Maybe you hear it, maybe you don't, but what is for sure is that deep in your heart space lives your truth.

Whatever is true for you in the many states you may have experienced in 2020, from; expansive exciting opportunity, perhaps a time to take a sacred pause, to an utterly devastating grief-stricken mindfuck (or any of these and every emotion in between!) We have been in this together, navigating a collective experience which we simply have no blueprint for. Yet individually, each one of us may be uncovering and revealing different truths long buried. We cannot deny that this year has seen the world confront truths that have never before been brought so glaringly under the spotlight, alongside the reinforcing of truths fundamental to the human experience.

In May, while most of the world was put under the strain of state enforced house arrest apparently for our own good, on the screens of our coveted devices we saw a black man, named George Floyd, brutally murdered by a white police officer. In lockdown we were a captive audience to this atrocity. For a moment, white people everywhere had a fleeting glimpse of the truth about life under Patriarchy for those who are not white. The world went into shock. Ardent battle cries that racism must end (which it really must) were voiced worldwide. We could speculate and stumble into Conspiracy-Ville about the interests of those who fund the BLM marches, but speculation aside, the truth was waiting to break out, exposing the dominance of Whiteness and its visceral impact on those it stops at nothing to control. The true horror of the police's institutionalised, racially-motivated violence continues. But we have all seen the truth now, it will not simply get back in its box and zip its inconvenient mouth like a good girl. Truth does not care about playing the agreeable game.

Truth and justice whispered in the UK news again towards the end of 2020. It was hinted that we may see white police officers held accountable for failings in securing the convictions of the racist white men who knifed Stephen Lawrence in 1993. I was eight when Mr Lawrence was killed in a racially-motivated attack in

South London. I saw his face on the BBC six o'clock news and listened to the plummy reporting voice. It didn't make sense. It sounded like he was just hanging out with a friend, and then he was dead. I asked my mum why they killed him because when you are eight you think grown-ups have all the right answers. Mum said, *'Because some white people hate black people.'* I didn't understand. I still don't. Heinous acts like the murder of black teenager, Trayvon Martin, in 2012, the murder of Breonna Taylor (shot by white police men just two months before Floyd was murdered) and the torture inflicted upon George Floyd expose the rotten racist guts of Patriarchy spilling out for all to see. The guts of a system which STILL sees fit to butcher black and brown bodies. I let my eyes take it in and then I turned off the news.

My truth says racism cannot end until Patriarchy ends. Until the hierarchies that decree which people are more worthy of life than others crumble into a billion pieces. Until the white institutions which profit from keeping the insanely rich insanely rich and choke the insanely poor into losing dignity by begging for food, choose people over profits and redistribute their wealth. Until the pharmaceutical industry stops experimenting on black and brown bodies in Africa and the East (yes Mr Gates I'm talking 'bout you and your 'vaccines'). Until the leaders of countries including England and the USA which stole people from Africa to sell as commodities simply hold their hands up and say, *'Yep, that was fucked. What the Hell were we thinking?! We are sorry. Here are your reparation payments and while we're at it, tell us what it has been like for you to have white people attempt to shit on you and your ancestors for generations. Let us feel your truth. Let us find counselling for all the Race-based Stress and Trauma that was inflicted. Show the world in your words, tell the truth in music, your art, your stories. Let us have it.'* When will that happen? The world waits on a pulsating inhale.

We saw yet again this year the ingrained deception that if you are male, white and in a position of power and domination, years of colonialism through Patriarchy gave you a free pass to inflict harm on people who do not look like you, ones you perceive as other. If you have power over another person, wear a police uniform (optional) and also happen to be visibly standing on his neck, you can reduce a man to cry out for his Mother, crying out for the one who gave him life to return for his final moments and comfort him through his transition to a place where racist BS does not exist. The place where there is only One. We all need the grace and comfort of the Divine Feminine Mother archetype this year, given what our eyes and souls have seen. I've needed to be comforted in the open, unconditional arms of the Wild. People have been seeping out into parks and fields drawn toward nature and the reliability of Her unending life and death cycles held by Mother Earth. Nature does not tell lies.

We were dosed more 2020 truth serum by Tara Reade, who courageously went public with her disclosure *alleging* Joe Biden sexually harassed and sexually *assaulted her in the early nineties. I had to write 'alleging'* because no charges have been brought against Biden. Let's be very clear; I believe Ms Reade. The US Democratic Party purport to "Believe Women" when we come forward to finally utter words that may have been keeping us prisoner for years; *'I was abused. I was assaulted. I was raped.'* I have spoken these words and felt the grief and unnecessary skin crawling shame of disclosing sexual violence. The voice of shame that wants to strangle self-compassion *'How could I let this happen? Why couldn't I stop it? If I hadn't been drunk, If I hadn't flirted......?'*

"Believe Women" was seemingly a message of solidarity to women who bravely spoke the truth of their pain caused by sexual violence while the stomach churning horrors of Weinstein's, Epstein's and Prince Andrew's rampages against underage girls and adults, burned into our psyche while disclosures stacked up. Except you won't be believed when you expose the truth that the Democratic presidential candidate is *allegedly* a sexual predator, same as his opponent. Sexual violence is a wound which does not heal in the dark. At some point the wound must be shown to the light of truth.

Sexual predators very seldom get convicted or even set foot inside court rooms. In England and Wales eleven women are raped every hour. That is the truth. More realistically, that's the truth we can extrapolate from those who feel able to officially disclose they were attacked. There are hundreds more who feel unable to tell police of their experiences. Nice going Patriarchy. This year revealed once AGAIN that if you are white, male and in a position of power you have a free pass to treat women as you please; including putting your sweaty hand up the collective work blouse, and of course much worse. Ms Reade told the truth and now her *alleged* perpetrator waits to be sworn in as president following 2020's election.

Yep, some women do lie about being sexually assaulted, but millions tell the truth. I told the truth of rape and sexual assault because I did not want to be part of the conspiracy that keeps women quiet or at best gaslighted when we tell the truth. I told the truth because I wanted my singular voice to help pave the way for the children who will need to disclose their abuse. I pray they will be believed. Tara Reade told the truth because she did not want to set the president (pun intended) for her daughter's generation to continue to live silenced. Sexual violence and the silence which it breeds is one of many wounds perpetrated by Patriarchy, for which the Feminine is the medicine. Feminine power is not power over but sovereignty and honouring of consent for all. Feminine power is sitting in silence and holding space for survivors to let their truth and trauma out bit by bit. The invasion of one's sacred body and the stealing of one's voice to speak the truth has been happening for time immemorial. More rape will happen, but more truth will out. I know that it will because something changed this year. People showed us they have had enough.

This is what I want you to know: Living Your Truth Is an Act of Resistance to the Patriarchy.

Truth is not always delivered by speaking your words aloud but may manifest as quieter 'autonomous aligned activism.' I got pinged by those words when waking up one morning recently. I had not slept well, it had been a night of fractured rest, but nevertheless those words came delivered to me by my Highest Self on a soft whisper of a thought. Autonomous Aligned Activism is not just doing whatever you want with no care for the consequences or impact on others. Nope, it is a state of being sourced by living Sovereign, powered by the soft (or loud!) voice of your truth. Autonomous Aligned Activism is making empowered choices for your life from your Highest Self also serving the highest good of those you care about.

2020 set the scene for many people to rise into their truth and cross the portal into Activism. It felt catalysing and inspiring. Take Marcus Rashford's rallying of the Conservative Party to demonstrate bare minimum humility by not stealing children's access to free school meals during the pandemic. The nation rose and collected hundreds of thousands of signatures to dissuade the Government's plan. We etched our names into online petitions, each quiet voice withdrawing consent from a system that enables child poverty, declaring; *Not in My Name.* We bore witness to the Sovereign actions of retired nurse Ylenia Angeli as she rescued her ninety-seven-year-old mother from a care home when the UK's second national lockdown was enforced. We bore witness to this grandmother suffering Dementia who was desperate to be with her family without being caged behind the care home windows. I wept and rooted for the Angeli family to make their escape with precious Grandma safely in the car. Ms Angeli was arrested for kidnap, her own mother returned by (anti)Social Services to the 'care' home. That primal truth-urge to connect with one's Mother line in times of crisis rises raw, time and again. And it will not stop. That Feminine urge to act from love even though it bends a couple of rules, rules so excruciatingly upheld by the jobsworth culture of The System. Autonomous Aligned Activism is demonstrated by acts of fierce love, truth and compassion, which ground us in one of many fundamental human/Divine truths; the act of giving a fuck about the suffering of others. Truth is, we have all suffered some way this year.

HIStory has rarely favoured truth tellers. Those who lift the veil, giving us a glimpse that things are not as they seem while shining light on to the abuses of power that have long dominated History, have time and again been met with at best ridicule and at worst, death. The searing truth of their lives snuffed out by hierarchical powers which attempt to bury truth in all her manifestations. They tried to burn all the truth tellers. Razing on pyres whole generations who chose to live life in reverence of the Earth and Her magic instead of bowing to an all seeing all judging Male Godhead. Wiping out the wise women, witches, initiates, teachers of the Mystery Schools, seers, healers, apothecaries, oracles and most of all the heretics who dared believe and practice a different truth. They lived the truth of sovereignty, discernment, knowledge of their inner wisdom found in altered states, of gnosis versus subjugation, control and power.

Their bodies were burned but their essence lives in each of us who choose to observe, question, discern and be autonomous to live our loving, aligned truth. That is the Sacred Feminine brand of truth. She who begins as a whisper when we feel something is that little bit off, misaligned from our truth that is inside us but is yet to be articulated, to being that Wild Creature lying belly down on the earth, pounding the ground with fists when her sovereignty is threatened, when choices over her own body are stripped, when consent is stolen. The Establishment has a penchant for abuse, for squeezing, censoring and choking the sound of truth. But the Feminine finds a way to slip free, snaking up, turning on Her heel to say: *Fuck Them. Enough now. Come reside with me where truth lives.* She won't stop telling HERstory.

She won't stop, even though we live in times when people are still killed for living their Truth. Modern Witch hunts. I sometimes have to pretend these things do not happen because it is not on my doorstep. It can be horribly distressing to consider the huge amount of human rights abuses and general maltreatment perpetrated by Patriarchy in the 21st century. People are murdered because they are not the right colour or the right gender or the right sexuality. People are imprisoned in concentration camps because the brand of patriarchy where they reside considers them the wrong religion, deemed parasitic to the nation they call home, subhuman and expendable. Remind you of anything? I felt overwhelmed earlier this year by the sheer amount of shit going down, the continued narrative of inhumanity. But something is shifting both in the micro and macro and I am optimistic…

Small acts of personal truth, like Ms Angeli's, are the elixir to the overwhelm which has been mounting this year. So earlier this year, I put my hand on my heart and began writing my truth. A book has been forming with my heart all over the pages. Truth on the page became medicine, cooling the fires of anger stoked by falsity on all the medias. I want you to feel the Truth Medicine too, it works.

Pull Down Your Mask,

Spit Out Your Gag,

Let Truth Reign.

SARAH WHEELER

Sarah Wheeler is an outspoken advocate for women recovering from the wounds of Patriarchy. She is a Reiki Teacher and Yoga Teacher specialising in Hatha Flow and Yoganidrā, Burlesque Performer, Author and (yoga geek!) founder of You're Enough Yoga in Hove, East Sussex.

She is in her biggest, juiciest joy when empowering women to uncover the medicine of deep rest through Yoga and Reiki, revealing the truth of being enough; just as we are. Her first book *Shadow and Rose: A Soulful Guide for Women Recovering from Sexual Violence* is published in 2021.

You can connect more deeply with her work at **www.youreenoughyoga.com**

2020'S LINE OF DESIRE
by Dainei Tracy

....

There is always a path that all of us, Gaia's creatures, naturally take when travelling. It is called the line of desire…or desire line.

It is the way that both the two leggeds and the four leggeds use to get from somewhere to elsewhere.

It might, or might not, be the shortest way. But it is usually the easiest way when viewed from above.

And it is always the way that is used most often. Well trodden. Easy to follow. My own line of desire runs by the side of my nearest wild, doing a modest approximation of the normal byway and highway, all tracked down and sign posted.

I'm sure I am mostly passing for human, but occasionally I know I slip upwards, not in a 'holier than thou' way, although, I have been accused… No… more directional or other dimensional. A lot of the time I have that flying feeling, coasting above it all, hovering with the buzzards, noticing the patterns, our lines of desire. Embodied in my soaring bird soul.

And flying above this place of 2020, because this year has the solidity of place. This time of 2020, is my eye, of the eagle of awareness, which is seeing that finally, finally there is a slowing… down …

into
…a
stopping.
…pause,

in all the newly revealed, yet older than old, and infinite, lines of desire of the whole of humanity. These are the ways we all are heading.

These are the paths we are inhabiting, in our unique times, in all our rainbow forms and crucified psychic spaces.

This potential pause can give us a bigger space and a deeper emptiness, that becomes a frame, the more it is looked at, that holds a lens. Suddenly throwing all that needs to be abandoned, in our behaviours and habits, into a sharpened relief.

What was just at the outer edges of our awareness, obscured by worry and busyness, or any agenda we choose to call our normal life, has swivelled round to centre view. Hasn't it?

And yes, I did say, 'needs to be abandoned'.

Yes. Needs to be.

Needs.

But, like what though? What needs to be abandoned? I am scared by this.

Me too, me too.

Abandoned sounds frightening. Let's sugar it up and say, 'let go of,' instead.

Maybe we don't know what we are really looking at here, though?

In which case I am saying that we are looking at the shapeshifting of the normal. To the way things have always been underneath.

To what supports us.

Below that which we subscribe to, below what we invest in.

To the mother in our underworld, deep in the centre, giving the heart of the world a little squeeze, just strong enough to be felt by everyone.

Little, that is, until she needs to squeeze a little harder.

Yes. Needs.

Because our normal is destroying itself and our Gaia, like a massive catapulting, thrashing, path-clearer through delicate leaf, branch, all the channels of life itself. By dumping its consequences all over this sacred ground. The beautiful, sacred, nourishing, sensitive ground that is actually our own selves in earthen form.

And all of this is criss-crossed, and woud about, with our very own unconscious lines of desire. Can we see what we are seeing here?

These lines we walk, and where we talk, and where we want to play and love.

By dumping this unexamined, yet normalised, cruelty, all through the etheric web of what is feelingly real, which is this reality of our own life force, flowing, responsive and miraculous. So knowing of what is consciously evolved and interconnected...do we trust it?

This exhausting, denying, normal, of fast this and fast that, accessible this and accessible that. This normal of covetable this and covetable that, fostering only lack. This normal that we all take refuge in.

We want things to go back to normal, do we?

...shovelling our eyes and ears and tongues into the funnels of paved over coercive civilisations, swallowing whatever we are presented with, completely unconnected to the rhythms of life. Normal.

Making us want to consume it more, eat all the pain of what we are doing, away, somehow, through the numbing wheels of addiction, and overdoing, into feeling nothing. No flow. This is the normal that Gaia will squeeze, when she needs to.

Need.

And all of this and that, worshipped as a godlike shadow, sitting astride our attention, riding our minds, while casting the biggest pool of suffocating dark in the whole of time and space, across our very souls.

Not 'them over there's' souls.
Our souls.
Because it is just us Gaian's here.

And we are all the ones who keep turning away from this truth.

Ploughing on in the furrows of our shortest, fastest routes to nowhere, slowly eroding the gift of the land and eating numbly into the edges of the sacred matrix that gives us our life. The hunger for attainment is ruling everything, but it is a false and wasteful way to use our attention when all is choked up around us, by us, and through us.

Creating more waste than we can safely and respectfully process right through the spectrum from material to psychological to spiritual, it is throttling the whole of creation.

And ruling these dysfunctional wounding systems with distracted robotic attention, so that this in turn ends up ruling us, causes… institutionalised murder, slavery and repression. Yes, well, we need to mention these death words… because these are the forces that fuel this desecration of life on our mother Gaia. And these are the things that need to be faced, that we need to be in relation with, before they can be transformational, evolving us up into our compassionate future.

Should we choose to see what we are seeing here.

This little slow down of 2020, this small squeeze, is a slim chance to do some of this facing up. To look back down behind us, seeing our own lines of desire. Our own maze of trodden paths. Which elsewhere are they bringing us to?

What kind of short cuts, and so called life hacks to greater material ease, have been eating our precious sensitive attention day after day?

And who have we trodden on to get to where we think we are?

Where are we coming from? What difference in the level of suffering have we really made to ourselves and others by chasing what we are being led to chase?

I mean, how conscious are we really?

We like to be underwhelmed so that we can continue chasing, so we can whip up some scheme and game it.

It's not very comfortable to be at the end of any of these lines having caught up with our quarry. Desire has been pumping and priming us for eternity and satisfaction has proved temporary. What the fuck do we do now?

Nobody in the beauty of this desert has arrived anywhere except in themselves in 2020. One way or another.

And some of us have always been aware of living here.

This might be you. Because some part of us all is conscious of everything that has surfaced at this dimly lit, yet deeply clear, fork in the path that is this year.

And let's clarify here, always having been aware of this pointless consuming, hasn't spoiled anything, or led to a life less lived, in fact, the light absorbed by the uninterrupted gaze of not subscribing to normal, can fully shift its beam to whatever needs to be seen at any time. And there is always something that needs to be seen.

Remember, this is our eagle eye of awareness fully engaged with what is being seen, by the one who is seeing.

This one that can see all those numberless infinitely long lines of desire and what they mean for us and our world.

We are this eye, the seer and the seen are one, and the revelation is that we don't really need this old normal any more.

It is only that it is up to us to take this seeing, capture our own attention and energy, and create more of the pause in the momentum of it.

To slow down the swift fritter of time spent being confused by all the conflicting messages from every time something or someone wants us to sell or buy, give or get. Do or not to do. Pulling our lines.

There is only one way to be in this marketplace of normal and that is with discernment and careful appraisal and knowing when something is naked, is of value, or inherently of no real importance.

This is the first step to being truly available to transformation and the evolving consciousness that feels like waking up at first, but sustains itself by actually never going to sleep. Our seed of wakefulness, that walks our path, that follows our intentional line of desire and tries and struggles, or pretends not to struggle.

That makes all this effort and cries out in stifled pain while pining after joy.

Us.

How is all this beauty and misery going to come together?

How do we actually respond to this dangerous, yet tender, squeeze of our collective heart from our real mother?

I know that my line of desire supports me and my part of the great transformation. I have quite often had to hide it to survive, but it has led me to this place like a magnet.

So I know that the way I respond moment to moment is the very transformation taking place. The way I respond and what I do and say and how I take my place in the normal without it taking hold of me, is my transformation. Which affects my field, my lines, my connections, you.

In the middle of what is unceasingly happening, now, finally there is a recognition in all the normal neighbourhoods of the world.

Maybe it's finally safe to land this ancient eagle body to do some real work? Maybe.

Because this is our mystery, all the solutions are yet to surface because we have more uncovering to do of what has become eroded beyond repair.

Of what has died forever.

Of what will be always lost to us when we are stuck being cogs in a machine that we built for our own security, and that is now busy killing anything that does not look like itself. Anything that does not feed it or buy from it. Anything that does not buy it at all. But what will feed us, then? The true nature of humanity? How will we survive? It will be these, our lines of desire. Connecting us, they criss-cross, they are the net of reality that Gaia has thrown over us with love, tightening and loosening, letting us know if we listen. Listen deeply, find and trust our own flows, bubbling up from earthen wells fed by Gaia herself as ourselves.

We are the ones that tread the paths, that generate the energy, that nourish the transformation. Let's find the words and the deeds that honour and validate what we have caused to disappear forever.

Let's create together this new language of tomorrow that doesn't need normal, which might just lead us into the rest of the 2020's with open hearts and willing souls, ready for the Gaia changes that are already in full swing, as she reaches out to us.

To, please, finally, recognise our ultimate inter-being.

Because walking this most sacred, precious, wild line of desire as far as it needs to go, has never been so needed as now.

Needs.
Yes.

We can only transform and become and face up to what is needed one step at a time, recognising the pull of the line of our desire and deciding when and where and how to pace who we are in the rhythm of the whole. Will it align more and more to the pulse of Gaia? Or will it align more and more to the machine of what has been normal, yet is so obviously insane.

What will we believe?

The eagle eye of our own awareness and the resilience of the eternal desert dweller? Or the false security?

DAINEI TRACY

Dainei shares practices from Yoga, Zen and Trauma psychotherapeutics, in which she is trained, and chosen for their supportive qualities. Offering one on one spiritual coaching, contactable through her website. **www.greatpeace.co.uk**

A dedicated pioneer of the mind, heart and spirit and an independent way finder of the hidden realms, she has long created disciplines and practices, from an early age, to help integrate life experience not accepted as the norm. With a passion for being free of indoctrination of any kind, she will support you in discovering the one who lives under all the conditioning, fear and suffering, often triggered by the systems we live within. This turning point in life is sometimes known as spiritual emergence(y).

You are the one, who is the change, that is needed now, today. Putting wisdom at its heart, using compassion as its fuel, it is the greatest honour to help create the energy fields that are the very birthing grounds of the evolution of consciousness.

2020 – RE-CLAIMING THE TRUE NATURE OF WHO WE ARE

by Angie Northwood

....

In February of this year, I attended a three-day writing retreat with five magical women. On our first morning together, we sat around a table adorned with Goddess oracle cards, and began to get to know one another, to explore what we were being called to write, to dive into the song of our souls.

I had initially resisted going to the retreat. I thought the resistance was that the setting did not resonate with me, I felt a contraction in my body when I looked at the details of the hotel, BUT, I knew the women going would balance this and my intuition was saying loud and clear, 'Go!'

And I did immediately feel held and loved by the beauty of the five magical women on our first morning together. We were already becoming soul sisters.

There was also something else going on too.

Next door was a room full of aged men, in suits, listening to other aged men in suits speaking at the front of their tidy rows and rows of seats. Sounds pretty innocuous perhaps. However for me, the energy coming from that room next door became overwhelming. It triggered something very deep in my soul. I began to feel fury, rage and grief racing through every cell in my body.

I began to shake and cry as I described my feelings of discomfort to my soul sisters. I told them how the men next door represented to me everything that has brought devastation to Mother Earth and to humanity. They represented the patriarchy – the old, tired, worn out systems and structures upheld by disconnected and damaged men, wounding and destroying and dismembering all of life. This was the real source of the resistance I had felt, the 'good girl' shadow asking, 'Who am I to think I can confront, challenge and dismantle the patriarchy through my writing?'

The book I was at the retreat to write was 'Re-Claiming the Crone,' so I was strongly 'plugged in' to the ancestral oppression of women by the patriarchy. The witch who was burnt at the stake was sitting beside me that morning, unafraid, potent and powerful.

Looking back at the strength of my feelings in that moment, I realise it was *the* moment in which I unknowingly, at a conscious level, sensed what was about to unfold in the world.

It was also the moment in which I began to step over the threshold into the initiation we were all about to experience; ready or not.

And so just a few weeks after the retreat, the UK was put into lockdown. The initiation had begun, the disintegration was beginning, the chaos and confusion was seeping into our lives.

Even here, in beautiful, safe, rural West Wales I felt confused about the virus and the growing restrictions. Was Covid-19 as deadly as we were being led to believe? Was it really unsafe to hug my neighbour who lives at the end of my track? Was it honestly dangerous to sit round the kitchen table and have a cup of tea with my best mate? How long was I going to have to hold onto my daughter's arm to stop her hugging other people, because there was no way she would understand through language. Would I be able to hold space for women again?

And at the same time, I breathed a sigh of relief. The frenetic, life-sapping, un-natural way of life for so many of us was being slowed, stilled, quietened.

As I began my journey into the unknown, I lost my will to write. I could not put pen to paper, no journaling, no notes, no thoughts and feelings that I could untangle, nothing would come. I couldn't find the words to express myself creatively. I needed time to be able to lift the veil in order to see with any clarity what was unfolding, what was being asked of me.

There was too an energetic overload, a scramble to replace the known and the comfortable with something else. I felt a need to fill the gaps, to find new ways to reach out and support others, new ways to stay connected, to stay in community, to feel that I still belonged. The only way to do any of that was to be online, a lot. Besides my family, Zoom became my primary source of being in relationship with others. This felt alien to me. I'm not particularly comfortable with technology, so I wanted to resist it, but I also needed it. I felt annoyance, inadequacy, left behind and a panic to be part of something. To 'do' something in response to the crisis.

The questions, the doubt, the anger, the grief, came and went, rolled in and out, took hold and dissipated almost on a daily basis for several months.

I am fortunate though, that through my writing, I belonged already to a community of soulful sisters online. Women who are creative, authentic, and connected to their wisdom. We gave space to one another to be heard, to be witnessed in our unravelling and vulnerability, in the sludgy, messy unknowing and in the crystal, clear clarity. We sisters allowed each other to explore our discomfort, to ask difficult questions, to cry, to rage and to be silent.

As we *all* grieved for the loss of human contact, in doing so, I connected ever more deeply to nature.

I am surrounded by nature; I chose to be so many years ago.

I experienced the healing power of nature when I arrived here in West Wales at the beginning of my menopausal journey and it was through relationship with Mother Earth that I learnt to welcome, embrace and fall in love with my own cyclical nature and becoming Crone. The alchemy of menopause, my transition and transformation, was an initiation; a death and re-birth experience. And *because* I had experienced *that*, I remembered that I was equipped to navigate the journey 2020 was taking me on.

I began to let go of my need to 'do' and surrendered into 'being.'

The land I live on is deeply nurturing and nourishing. I feel my ancestors in the land. There is magic and wisdom here which roots me and grounds me, and at the same time connects me to spirit, through the elements, through the birds and the bees, the tree's and the stream, the sky, the moon and the stars. The land helped me to hear the quietening of the world, to feel the collective slowing and stopping. Within that spaciousness I heard the whispering of my ancestors, 'We are here. We are holding you.'

So, I spent my days in conversation with the land, listening to her wisdom, being reminded of why I had chosen to be here. And because we could not work, Rob, my husband, and I had space and time together to revisit the vision and dreams we had brought with us when we moved from the city. We planted new crops for food in the polytunnel *together*. The woodland we had planted together, we were now coppicing *together*. We had more time to play, to dance, to talk and just to be. And when grief or anger or fear nudged us, we looked at them and shared our thoughts and feelings with each other.

On these days I felt blissful.

The days became weeks, in which I found great joy. Through being in alignment with the rhythm of nature, I became excited and hopeful for a new world to be birthed. I rejoiced for nature while she rested and healed from the greed and destruction of human behaviours.

There was too, the polar opposite of this. Stepping out of alignment and into the vibration of fear as we were told death tolls were rising and no sight of restrictions being lifted. I chose not to listen constantly to the news, something I had allowed myself to be sucked into in the early days of lockdown. I listened less and less, and then not at all, feeling the anger rise whenever I did, ending always with me shouting at the radio. It felt unhealthy, pointless, and submissive to listen to what I increasingly believed to be distorted truths at best and blatant lies at worst from the people controlling us. There were days when I felt utter despair. My body, heart and soul ached for those people living with abuse, with hunger, with violence, trapped in their homes, no access to support, no way out.

The question I kept returning to was, 'How do we change this?' 'What part do I need to play in creating the change?'

As we each witnessed the world falling further and further away from love and relationship as a result of being isolated from one another, forbidden to touch one another, left to die alone, children separated from parents, access to healthcare and to earning a living eradicated, the layers of grief I felt manifested into the physical.

I had been feeling some discomfort in my left breast for many months. I realised just recently, it had in fact been since March, when we went into lockdown. I became fearful that I had breast cancer and having learnt from past dis-ease in my body, I understood that my heart space, the centre of how we feel and express love and relationship, was giving me a message to pay attention to, to be curious about, to have the courage to look at what was going on. The thought of maybe having cancer was inviting me to look at death; my own and the death of the world as we know it. I had no desire to die at this time, but I felt surprisingly calm thinking about it. I honestly thought, 'If this *is* my time to go, so be it.' What my body guided me to do was to stay in connection with my heart space, to stay in connection with my intuition, to stay grounded in connection with Mother Earth and in so doing, follow the thread of my ancestral wisdoms, the voice of the feminine rising, the call to raising the vibration of love in the world through healing the patriarchal wounding.

And so, within *that* container, I began to sit in ease with both the known and the unknown.

The unravelling of what I had felt safe in, the poke to look at my own mortality and the necessary death of our world structures *before* we can experience our collective transformation, ignited a beautifully spacious focus for journeying, visioning and dreaming; these becoming a source of joy, insight and creativity, bringing me back always to Mother Earth and hearing the messages she offers to us.

She shows us we are inseparable.

She shows us that everything must die.

She shows us re-birth.

She shows us the abundance we can share when we are in a caring relationship of reciprocity with each other.

I have received so many beautiful messages from nature over these past eight months.

I go to my soulful space down by the stream, I sit on the bridge dangling my legs and feet just above the icy water and dream into the flow. I am in love with what Mother Earth teaches me. I see in the water, even as the stream flows, there are spaces of stillness where the water is held by the bank and boulders and fallen branches. Within the stillness is the dark, an invitation to be quiet, to reflect, just as the tree's and sky are reflected in the water. I notice how the water moves around the boulders and stones, bubbling, stirring, taking debris with it as it moves on and on and on.

I see too how clear the water is and how the shapes beneath hold no form as she endlessly flows over them; the stones and shingle, reeds and foliage seem to shapeshift, but are only really changed over time and time and time, from the gentle touch of the water.

Just as nature takes time to grow, change, disintegrate and be born anew within her never-ending cycles, so it will take time for humanity to change; it will take time for us to shapeshift into more conscious beings. We are yet to witness the full death part of the patriarchy. There is still so much healing to be done. There is still so much re-membering to happen.

It is time.

Time for us to be courageous in our vulnerability and step over the threshold, into the portal of a new paradigm of healing and love.

When we have collectively re-wilded ourselves, when we have re-claimed the true nature of who we are, when we raise our vibration to resonate with the heart-beat of Mother Earth, when we open our hearts and align to the song of our souls, it is *then* that we will see, feel, live, in love, in peace, in harmony with Mother Earth and one another.

That is my dream. That is my hope.

I will leave you now with the words I wrote that morning back in February; it was written for women in that space and time, the words are now also lovingly for men.

Honouring my Sisters

Let me hold this space for you,
I am holding space for you
I will witness you
I will honour your courage
My tears will fall and flow with yours
You are not alone dearest one
Look behind you
You will see them all
Your sisters, your ancestors standing strong
Hand in hand, in hand in hand
Let us catch you as you fall
We are holding space for you,
For your rage, your pain, your grief
For your undoing, your searching, your discovering
We will dance with you around the fire of your
disintegration
We will enter the cave with you and hear your wailing
your laughter and your joy
We will lay naked with you
As you crawl, re-birthing from the Earth
You are reclaiming that which was stolen from you my love
You are rewilding the true nature of who you are.

ANGIE NORTHWOOD

Angie Northwood lives in beautiful rural West Wales with her husband and two adult children. She holds space for women who wish to re-claim and re-wild the true nature of who they are. Angie's work is grounded in the female cyclical nature, her deep connection to Womb Wisdom, the song of her soul and to Mother Earth. She is also an author, her first book being *Take Off Your Armour and Have a Cup of Tea.*

Find out more at:
www.spiralsofwellbeing.co.uk

2020 – YEAR OF TRANSCENDENCE
by Sarika Jain

....

On January 1st of 2020, as I lay in bed next to my one-month old infant, I asked the universe for a sign for what I could be focusing on for my work. Although I didn't feel like I needed to continue working right away, I felt something was emergent, a different emanation of myself was being midwifed, and I had a creative spark flowing through me. I had just had a profoundly ecstatic delivery with a beautiful baby girl and was floating in the liminal space of new life being birthed in the middle of winter. I was in the midst of a mystery unfolding, a new possibility, in between moments of delirium from sleep deprivation and sheer exhaustion.

I witnessed the moment of pushing the baby through the 'ring of fire' with no epidural support, wondering if I would even survive, wanting the baby to stop thrusting forward yet praying for the pain to end. I pushed with all my might, roaring like a lion, with my husband and doula by my sides, being coached and cheered on by a team of doctors, nurses and midwives, and within moments, a miracle happened – the birth of my daughter, Maya, and the possibility of the indescribable joy in experiencing motherhood all over again.

Thankfully, this time I had managed to escape postpartum depression which was an unfortunate cornerstone after my first delivery.

That delivery had torn me apart, physically, emotionally, physiologically. While the delivery itself was immensely challenging, I felt heartbroken as I watched my hormones ravage my body like brushfire, eating up my willpower, exposing me to anxiety attacks I had never felt before. Despite the discomfort, I pushed to care for myself and the baby, going from crying to laughing within minutes due to the intensity and ups and downs.

When the postpartum period was finally over, I was elated, and I chalked up my journey into motherhood as a spiritual fire walk, a crossing through the dark night of the soul that allowed me to transcend to the echelons of warriorhood. It also grounded me in empathy and deep connection to the feminine consciousness, which entails serving life while feeling deeply vulnerable, and a new appreciation for the role of the masculine in my life, seeding and supporting the creation rumbling through me.

....

As I sat with what was emergent, I realized I wanted an avenue for creative self-expression and to find a sense of truth within me; something outside of being engaged in the world as I had in the past. What was the wild, authentic desire within me that I could access in this primal, shamanic portal I was walking through? What was the birth that was happening, yet again?

When I sat with the emotion I desired to feel in 2020, the feeling that came up was *Transcendence*.

Transcendence for me has had a *hoity-toity* connotation, reserved for spiritual aspirants and yogis, people who lecture on mindfulness or spend their free moments on beaches meditating and doing asanas. This seemed out of reach for a new mother waking every three hours to feed a ravenous, inconsolable child. How could I revel in this vibrational realm, while being present during the very human act of mothering, which sometimes was deeply uncomfortable and requiring every ounce of my attention and energy? On the flipside, I also could see that being pregnant, giving birth and caring for a child, primitive activities that required tremendous presence and love, had given me a unique opportunity to be *undone*, and allow whatever is authentic to me to unravel.

When I tuned into the feeling of transcendence, there appeared to be a golden radiance, a feeling of upliftment, an elevation beyond my current state, a revelation of some sort. A knowing that I am in the world, but not of it. It evoked in me a greater sense of heart openness, a wonder with the world and delicious acceptance of being. Of fully experiencing pain and pleasure, but not attaching to either. Of accessing a deeper truth and luminosity, which appeared easily during the mundaneness of life of mothering, yet was also fleeting.

....

Years before 2020 began, during my first pregnancy, I started having panic attacks at random moments. When I would be in the subway or elevator while traveling from my apartment in New York City, I would be gripped by immense claustrophobia; and sometimes would feel leery or insecure at night or while walking around. My body was telling me something through these panic moments when I felt paralyzed and felt a quickening of my heart rate and corresponding adrenaline rushes – was it a grief that I hadn't processed? I envisioned I was entering a long, underground tunnel, and was stuck with the walls caving in, the same feeling I have when I am about to deliver a child.

If I were honest, I had intuitively felt that the world would be changing drastically, and it was feeling even more imminent. *There would be a death and rebirth of some sort; there was no way out.* I worked with a hypnotherapist who helped me overcome my fear of darkness and closed spaces that had escalated due to hormonal surges in my body. By the grace of God and through this man's help, I was able to be comfortable with the darkness more, despite my fear of uncertainty of what was to come.

....

The very next morning, after sending that missive to God asking me for direction in my work, I got onto social media and saw advertisements related to publishing one's book. I thought somewhat sceptically, "Maybe I'm supposed to write a book? God, I need more proof here!" The same day, I got an e-mail from an old mentor who told me that she envisioned me becoming a writer; and later that afternoon during grocery shopping, I spoke with my husband about what to prioritize for work, he confirmed that he, too, felt this was the time to write a book. Third time's the charm, they say, when it comes to synchronicity!

I began to feel into writing a book. It seemed particularly challenging given the little time I had between childcare and recovery, yet, it was the perfect, solitary, creative activity for a new mama. Writing was a seed that was planted in me from my childhood, always looking for an opportune time to sprout, and somehow, now seemed the time.

As fortune would have it, the very next day, I received an e-mail from Nicola Humber talking about joining a Writing Mastermind. My heart raced as I read it, and I took the plunge.

The year 2020 began with this endeavor – of writing a book, being in the mystery of life, while attending to everyday responsibilities of childcare and recovery. I knew I wanted *something* to transform, but what was it? I had a feeling that writing would be my container for alchemy.

At first, I did not know what my book would be about and each day, I simply wrote in a stream of consciousness whenever I could get a moment. I attended group calls with other women in which we shared our joys and trepidations about our writing journeys.

The tides changed soon enough. The news of the Coronavirus started floating from China and Europe, keeping us glued to the news. When would it arrive, and what would the impact be? Would it be deadly? Would we lose our loved ones? Would New York City be so lucky as to somehow avert the disaster?

The second weekend of March, we decided to visit my in-laws in New Jersey for a couple of nights. On the train ride there, we heard about the first documented case in New York City. By the end of the weekend, over a hundred tested positive. *'What should we do? Do we even travel back home by train?'* we wondered. In that moment, a good friend told us to simply stay put, and not go back, out of compassion for all.

Not go back to our home! What a wild thought, and yet, we decided that in that moment, there could be no other answer.

Much like the labor process of birth, life began to take on a life of its own and we had to surrender. There was so much uncertainty and excitement at the same time. We moved into communal living, with my mother-in-law supporting in childcare and cooking while I scurried after a three-month-old and a three-year-old. My body ached and I mustered through with fragmented sleep. My husband quickly shifted gears to managing his team and clients virtually, holding space for his employees' fears and questions.

As all this was occurring, I sat with the waves of discomfort, which came over me like contractions. I grieved about a lost past and an uncertain future, knowing that this would be the point of no return that my body was signalling to me. There were moments when I grappled with fear. What would happen to my husband's job, to our family and friends in big cities, to our parents who were vulnerable, or our relatives who were doctors? I wondered if it were the last time that I would see my loved ones in person, and even faced the fear of getting sick myself, or possibly losing my own husband.

Despite all of this, I felt strangely calm, sensing that all of this was a natural part of life, that what had felt like labor pains was now coming to a culmination, that somehow we are now passing through the ring of fire as humanity was potentially giving birth to something new, unseen before.

As a mother, I grieved for the world, holding the pain, truly understanding for the first time the meaning of the phrase, "the only way out, is through." I also felt love and compassion emanating from my heart, deeply recognizing the sacredness of every single person on this planet, feeling my connection to everything. I prayed for healing and transcendence of suffering, not just for the pandemic, but for all of our collective trauma till now. What new life would we live, after passing through this portal? Would the world as we know it end? What is it like to hold space for something to emerge naturally, and hopefully for the better, through our collective human experience?

....

In this setting, writing took on an even greater sense of importance. It proved to be a spiritual raft that helped me feel sane and witness my own thoughts and experience. I was dancing with fleeting creative impulses while learning to navigate a new viscerally uneasy yet trusting connection with the divine.

Miraculously, a new reality birthed itself around me. As I gestated with the book in my womb, my nest was being created (as I imagine it) by celestial birds and elemental beings working while I slept. The house next door to my in-laws opened up which we bought, bringing to fruition a long-held dream of creating an intentional community and living close to our loved ones. We became close with our neighbors with whom we leaned on during both joyful and tumultuous times. I spent every moment I could outdoors, smiling with the sun streaming on my face, catching butterflies and counting ants with my little ones, whom I otherwise would have sent to daycare. My husband started growing a little garden and we became crafty in the kitchen, serving elaborate lunches and dinners and capping our day with small celebrations. My parents flew in from India to stay with us for the foreseeable future. In a way, everything I had dreamed about was coming to fruition, made possible due to impermanence.

My life, in these turbulent times, was somehow aligning with what resonated deeply with my heart and soul.

....

Motherhood sometimes requires so much patience that it becomes a superhuman quality. Due to the vulnerability of the role, it also invariably leads to a great deal of humility and surrender. Mothers are shamans in the know of the mystical process of creation, and have firsthand experience in the lovemaking, seeding, conception, gestation, labor, delivery and postnatal care for this delicate, wondrous process. While they are masters at the secrets of creating and sustaining life, they also recognize that life is only possible because of death; a new sprout can only bloom if something else has already been composted. There is a sacredness to the duty of serving life and death which engenders courageous warriorship driven by a sense of fierce love. Being around young ones, however, reminds mothers to have an absurd lightness and humor with it all.

Mothering requires one to have an innate trust in life, that despite all our machinations, there is a creative force moving through that can't be stopped. While bringing a child into the world, you have to trust that your body has the natural intelligence to complete the process, like an acorn destined to become an oak tree.

The only thing you can pray for, is the guidance and support to help you move through with wisdom, compassion and grace. You watch as your world falls apart, your body ravaged and your belief system collapses. The ego will hold on for dear life, hating the changes. You will grieve and wrestle with life. Yet if you're able to hold space for the discomfort and understand the revelatory process of death and creation, you can be a part of ushering in something greater, perhaps even miraculous. You'll be able to touch into your personal truth of who you are and witness the awesome paradox of an awareness that you are both nothing and everything.

As I'm penning this, I'm in the labour process of writing my book. I have a loving group of women helping me midwife my book, along with my eternal companion and champion, my husband, by my side, holding my hand as I wade through waves of both ecstasy and painful contractions while *something* is being birthed. What, when or how are out of my hands, and all I can do is show up, be a mother, knowing that death and emergence are around the corner.

I see the world changing around me, old systems and structures falling apart, and people having to choose what to fear, love or trust. Watching the breakdown, I wonder, as I had moments before my daughter popped out of me, 'Will we break through?' I pray that my writing and beingness will, in some way, support the nascence of the baby that desires to be born, as we pass through this collective ring of fire.

SARIKA JAIN

Sarika Jain is a leader in love strategy and transformational coaching and is the creator of the Sacred Soulmate System: 5 Steps to Finding 'the One.' Her unique approach encompasses everything from uncovering relationship patterns and closing one's 'Ex Files' to practicing self-love and mindfulness while dating, all with the goal of inspiring women to live the lives they've dreamed about – experiencing profound love, success and fulfilment.

Sarika's background includes working in the corporate world and on Wall Street for over fifteen years before deciding to pursue her dream full time of creating a movement around healthy love and empowerment for women nearly ten years ago. She is a student of energy healing, psychology, feminine leadership and relationships. She's been called a "Relationship Sorceress" by her clients.

She lives in New Jersey with her husband and two young daughters, and leads a joyful, intentional life, focused on community building.

Find out more at **www.sarikajain.com**

ARRIVING IN **MY** BLACK BODY
by Lola Fayemi

....

I always knew I was black, but to be honest I just felt like Lola. I'm a black British woman of Nigerian descent. My parents were raised in colonial Nigeria and came to London back in the 60s and 70s for a better life.

I navigated my life as a black person in England in a very individual way. Thankfully, I'm good with people. I'm smiley, funny, bright and intelligent. I kept my head down, did what I was told and was able to (largely) follow the rules. I was also fortunate enough to be born and raised in multicultural South London and not the English countryside where I would be the only black person for miles.

Becoming a Mother at 31 was a game changer for my identity. Not only was I grappling with my new identity as a Mother, my racial identity was also evolving. I now had a beautiful black boy to raise in this world and for the first time, I was forced to think beyond myself racially. As a baby he was a real cutie. I started becoming aware that the same people who were raving about how cute he was, would one day be scared of him, clutching their bag closer to their bodies as he passed them in the street.

He was eight years old when I first had to tell him about the reality of racism. I really resented having to tell him, but I knew I would be negligent in my responsibilities as a parent if I didn't. It was heartbreaking, I felt like I was bursting my beautiful son's bubble of innocence as I explained to him that there were people in the world that didn't expect much of him because of the colour of his skin. I didn't want to but I had to tell him. I couldn't send him out there over-exposed to experience it for himself, for him to then internalise it as something being wrong with him. NOTHING was wrong with him. The issue was with the world and the oppressive systems we all live in.

Systems that need us to be out of our bodies to live within them. Systems that require us to dissociate or medicate ourselves to cope with them. Systems we accept, tolerate and adhere to as 'the norm' despite the inhumanity of them. Systems whose standards we have all internalised. Systems that are ripe for dismantling and that dismantling starts within us, in our bodies. Arriving in your body is a key step of the real revolution that needs to happen to dismantle these oppressive systems.

....

I first consciously arrived in my ancestral body during a constellations workshop in 2014. Constellations are a powerful, systemic method for revealing hidden dynamics within and between people. In the one I took part in, an external map of my inner world was recreated through other people tapping into and embodying the systemic intelligence of my field.

I had no conscious idea of what I was taking part in. My intention was to attend the course to increase my systemic knowledge and manage my team more effectively. How wrong was I?

I ended up spending the morning in floods of tears as I released generations of trauma in my Mum's side of the family. I had the deep visceral experience of fully feeling and letting go of intense emotional pain I was carrying which wasn't mine. It was truly one of the most profound experiences I've ever had and it set off a healing that rippled through my family for the years to come.

I first consciously arrived in my physical body during my Nia white belt training in 2015. Nia is a mind and body dance conditioning programme that helps you break patterns in your body and embody joy. The previous year was basically one big ongoing trigger for me as I was waking up to the fact I was carrying childhood and ancestral trauma. I was riddled with feelings of insecurity that just wouldn't shift. I didn't know where they were coming from or what was happening to me.

I was leading a project that was pioneering coaching for young men in prisons and we had won an innovation grant from the Ministry of Justice. I designed a transformational leadership coaching programme and trained 14 Coaches to lead it at two notorious London prisons. We also pioneered a large systemic workshop for an entire wing at another London prison. It was a year of meaningful, incredible and purposeful work that was completely soul-led. But I was also working with the darkest and most traumatic system in our society and it was vicariously triggering the fuck out of my unresolved and underlying trauma.

My body was repeatedly hijacked by the trauma so I knew it had to be resolved somatically. I started Somatic Experiencing sessions and decided to do my Nia white belt training to support the processing of the frozen feelings through movement.

The white belt was one of the hardest things I've ever done. I felt so much resistance it was insane. I felt like Goldie Hawn in the first half of 80's film Private Benjamin, something within me was throwing the biggest tantrum! It was so emotionally painful for me. It was like all the darkness within me surfaced at the same time. And then, more than halfway through, the breakthrough montage moment (like in a film) happened and I felt myself arrive in my body.

The Joy! I was in my body and it was like my spirit just clicked into place in my body. My body felt free and blissful. I was listening to her and she was speaking to me, it was incredible. *Oh yes, I could live like this!*

Only I couldn't.

It still wasn't safe enough for me to stay in connection with my body yet. I still needed to dissociate.

Even though I couldn't maintain the Nia, I was happiest on a Salsa dance floor and regularly danced. By Salsa, I mean the roots of the dance – Afro-Cuban Salsa not the sanitised Salsa of Strictly or Dancing with the Stars. Afro-Cuban Salsa dancing is a deeply joyful, fun and meaningful experience for me. From the outside I may appear to be doing rum shots and having a laugh. But inside it's a somatic reclamation and celebration of the Yoruba culture of my ancestors, before colonisation and the transatlantic slave trade.

....

I first consciously I arrived in my black body in 2020. I felt that familiar sense of activation after the murder of George Floyd. I recognised the feeling. I'd felt it after the London Riots in 2011 which led to me working with prisons.

I couldn't watch the video, I didn't need to. Like millions of black people in the world, I knew exactly what this was. We'd been through this so many times before, it was not a surprise to us. You know that symbolic image of Trayvon Martin? It sometimes glitches in my mind when I see my son in a hoody – this shit's been very real to us for a long time.

After 9/11 as the islamophobia was ramping up, I asked a friend whose family were from Pakistan how it felt to be Muslim? She answered, "I feel even more Muslim." I recalled this in the days following George Floyd's murder because suddenly, I'd never felt more black.

A fire started to rise up in me and with it the word 'ENOUGH.' ENOUGH of colluding with a system that is not built for me and is trying to destroy me. ENOUGH to playing the lame white moderate's game. And ENOUGH to being stopped dead in my tracks by white fragility. I'm beyond caring who is upset by this. Your tears and discomfort do not have a higher value than the lives of my brothers and sisters.

It was time to step out of the frequency of white fragility and colour blindness and take a stand as the Warrior Queen I truly am. I knew white fragility would be the biggest barrier, it always had been. We've all been calibrating to the frequency of white fragility – a dangerous, toxic and destructive upholder of white supremacy.

As black people, we're always (consciously or unconsciously) aware that we're scary to white people and we shouldn't scare them. We're too loud, aggressive, passionate, angry – our food's even too spicy goddamit! Consequences of scaring white people range from being judged as being rude to losing your life. I'm less bothered by racist name calling, that's harmful but a distraction. What bothers me is the institutional and systemic racism that holds back billions of people every single day and led to the murder of George Floyd. I see a straight line from fragility to his murder. No excuses, it's time for us to calibrate to our power not our wounds.

I have a particular lens that I look at the world through. It's a mash-up of social justice, spirituality, psychology/ therapy/personal development and somatic intelligence. My work has always had an awareness of context. The systems we all live within – patriarchy, white supremacy and capitalism – affect us ALL, mostly negatively. Even if you're favoured by them, the power you have under them is pure illusion.

Discovering Cultural Somaticist Resmaa Menakem this year gave me more language for what I already knew to be true. Resmaa speaks of white, black and blue (police) bodies and the trauma they all carry. According to Resmaa THIS is what perpetuates racism and THIS is where we need to dismantle it, at the level of the body.

A lightbulb went off! It all made sense....

When my white dance teacher talked about how hard it was for her to learn to move her chest in particular way in Afro-Cuban dancing. I found it easy but she was a trained dancer so I thought maybe I was doing it wrong. But it was easy for me because it's culturally how my ancestors moved, that memory lives in my body.

When I was doing my Nia white belt training and was told to let my body move out of time to the music as a form of expression it was felt wholly unnatural and wrong to me. It felt as bad as when the midwife told me not to push during labour despite my son being cooked and ready to come out.

This year it dawned on me that ALL of my coach training has been created and delivered within the systems of white supremacy and the patriarchy – systems that weren't built for me. Or I should say, not built for me to thrive in!

I'm a Coach, I've been a Coach since 2007. Coaching is an amazing transformational tool that I love but something has always felt off for me with the industry. Truthfully, I find my profession to be largely immature and simplistic. I have always felt like an outlier as a Coach. I liked it because I didn't want to lumped into the same category as most Coaches who, in my opinion, lacked nuance, cultural awareness and the capacity that comes from a healthy and robust nervous system.

I hold Coaches to a higher standard than most people because we are working with people, about being people. This is an honour and a privilege that I take seriously. I have my own crew of Coach friends that I trust and love, but the industry as a whole can do one. I could never put my finger on what it was that rubbed me up the wrong way – until this year.

Being bound by the standards that come with white bodies doesn't work for me. White supremacy is fuelled by colour blindness. It sounds noble on the surface doesn't it to say 'I don't see colour' but it upholds the system of white supremacy. Colour blindness shuts down conversation on identity, robbing us of access to key sources of our authentic power.

Also, 'I don't see colour,' means you don't see me because I am not the same as you. I see colour, I see difference and I love it.

'We're all the same,' diminishes and gaslights people of colour because we know that we're not all the same. We don't want to all be either. We know that really means you want us to be like you. We don't want to be like you, it doesn't look that appealing to us. We want to be us.

Culturally I'm a hybrid. British in some ways, African in others, South London for the rest. I'm loud, colourful, vibrant, direct, straight-talking, boundaried, fierce and I like my humour of the harsh side…. I have no desire to be repressed, contained, 'nice', seething inside, scared of conflict and disingenuous – yes this is how I feel pressured to be, under the gaze of white supremacy.

Generally speaking, white bodies cannot handle discomfort in the same way that black bodies can, hence the rush to positivity and the spiritual bypassing. But it is in that dark discomfort that the transformation happens. How can you hold space for someone going through that if you can't be with it yourself? I've also seen many white coaches wax lyrical about things they know nothing about, yet still feel completely entitled to have an opinion on. Things like anxiety, depression, trauma, cultural bias etc. Unconsciously creating harm whilst believing they're creating safe spaces. We can do better than this.

Landing in my black body as a Coach this year means speaking MY truth. Not just for me but because as a minority in my profession it's important for my voice to be in the mix. It means acknowledging the bias towards whiteness and masculine energy (even in a predominantly female profession), means that a lot of what is promoted doesn't actually apply to me which is why it feels off. It means valuing that I can hold space for bigger and deeper transformations because my capacity is greater than the industry standard. And I do not need to dilute my work to fit it into a shallower mould.

It means acknowledging that phrases like *'shine your light,'* *'unleash yourself,'* and *'be unapologetically you,'* bring up deeper fears for black people and people of colour who have generally had to 'hide' important parts of ourselves to survive or get ahead.

So 2020, from the bottom of my heart, I thank you for bringing me home to myself in a bigger way. I have no idea what happens next but I'm in……

Over to you 2021!

LOLA FAYEMI

Lola Fayemi is a Transformation Specialist, Leadership Coach & Writer.

She works with Cycle Breakers who are pioneering new ways in their life, family, business or work. Leaders who are taking a stand for something bigger than themselves led by the stirrings of their soul. Lola supports them in owning their power, living a life in alignment with their authentic self and living their truth not their conditioning.

She is currently writing her first book, 'Sovereignty: Live Your Truth Not Your Conditioning,' which will be out in 2021.

You can find her at
www.bossassliving.com or follow her
@bossassliving on Instagram.

AN ANGEL'S PRAYER
by Carrie Myers

....

With tattered wings
And tarnished halo
She sits crossed legged
Atop a rocky ledge

She drops her head into her hands
She weeps
Weeps for the heartache
Weeps for the pain
Weeps for the loss

Allowing it all to flow through her
And down her face
The tears ebbed over the rocks
Down into the ravine
Forming a puddle,
A pond
Then a lake of tears

How many souls has she tried to comfort?
How much agony she has absorbed
Hearts she sought to comfort
She has lost count

The world is overwhelmed with hopelessness, anger
and pain
Her tribe of angels are exhausted, battered and bruised
Fighting the resistance of hope, peace and love

She longs for those days
She will feel clean, refreshed, healed and energized
Leaving the sadness, anguish, sorrow and scars behind
As she held the last soul gently, lovingly in her tired arms
She felt a chill from their very being
She noticed her feathers falling to the earth
As her heart sank broken, shattered
Her body quaked

Tighter, she held this soul
Hoping to squeeze the pieces back together
But the resistance prevailed

Tears cascading from her eyes now~
Growing the lake at the bottom of the ravine
Her mind racing to unearth any remaining hope
Left in this world

It has to be here
Somewhere in the souls of those who remain

Her last tear fell, as human pain was released from her grip
She wiped her face with her threadbare gown
Looking bleary at the horizon, once again

Then down at her earthen feet
Her head dropped in prayer
Her knees fell to the rocks
Her pleas echoed in the darkness

She clenched her hands tighter
She spoke the words of love and hope from her
crippled heart
She willed hope, peace, love, joy and tenderness
To engulf this weary world
She squeezed her eyes so tight that, even they resisted
But released one last tear to fall

Her hands clasped her chest
Her knees cringed from the shards of broken dreams
that littered her perch
Shivering and fearful of the overwhelming darkness
She slowly opened her eyes

Then, there it was
That tiny shimmer emerging from the peak of a distant
mountain

She blinked furiously
She sensed a shift
She felt the resonation from the other angels' prayers

Hope, Light, Unity, Peace
Was tiny and still very fragile
But it was there

She heard the chatters as the angels began to gather
The sounds of cherished resilient spirits
The darkness will begin to lift

The hearts will begin to open to hope, change and love
Her heart pounded with elation

Suddenly, she noticed her wings began to bloom and
straighten
Her gown rinsed clean
Her feet no longer muddy
Her hands no longer bruised

Although the chill still engulfed her
She could begin to feel the warmth
The sun emerging through the clouds, storms and
darkness

Her prayers and those of her Angel Tribe
Have been heard, held and answered
The Human Spirit will once again begin to shine.

CARRIE J MYERS

Carrie J. Myers, a native of Asheville, NC, and mother of three, has been writing since she was 10 years old. Most of her work is poetry, which reflects the phases of her life and helped her process her journey along the way.

As a yoga instructor, she discovered new ways to dig deep into her subconscious, pulling from her practice, the words that held higher meaning and growth. As she puts her work out into the world, she hopes to inspire change in the hearts and souls of her readers, while holding space for each interpretation to resonate with each soul's purpose.

Carrie is passionate about creating and recognising the beauty in the mess that life can throw at us, at times. Her goal is to help readers to rediscover their authentic selves and revive, create and discover their light within.

Connect with Carrie at:
www.instagram.com/cjmyerspoet/

ABOUT THE UNBOUND PRESS

....

The Unbound Press is a soul-led publishing imprint, committed to working with female authors whose writing activates a feeling of deep connection and transformation in others.

Movements such as #MeToo have shown us the power of womxn coming together and sharing their stories.

And if there's one thing we're certain of, it's that in these tumultuous and transformational times, the world NEEDS your magic.

We honour the right of all beings to be their fullest, freest selves and to write in a way that expresses that.

At The Unbound Press we're turning the traditional publishing model on its head. We provide a platform for diverse voices, for authors to express their unique stories and the truest essence of what they're here to share at this time.

We truly believe that we can change the world, one book at a time. Are you in?

Find out more at: **theunboundpress.com**

Feeling the call to write the book you're REALLY here to write and want to do that in creative community? Find out more and join the Unbound Writing Mastermind at: **nicolahumber.com/the-unbound-writing-mastermind**